This Book

This book by Bishop Robert E. Joyce offers you revelatory insights what to do when you have obeyed God, but still find yourself asking, "Where is He?"

You will learn what to do when your faithfulness seems "rewarded" with adversity--confusing and difficult circumstances. As we explore the word of God throughout this book, it will activate the anointing within us and stir us to advance the Kingdom of God.

This book will help you process your experiences according to God's word and His way. Rather than panic, you will learn God's ways of developing your character and integrity; and conforming you to the image of Christ.

No longer will you be moved by your emotions. You will be moved by your assignment!

Welcome to boot camp, Warrior!

Handling Life's Hardships

First Aid For Life's Difficulties

Bishop Robert E. Joyce

Copyright © 2016 by Bishop Robert E. Joyce

No part of this publication may be reproduced, stored in a retrieval system, or transmitted in any form by any means—electronic, mechanical, digital photocopy, recording, or any other without the prior permission of the author.

All rights reserved solely by the author. The author guarantees all contents are original and do not infringe upon the legal rights of any other person or work. No part of this book may be reproduced in any form without the permission of the author.

Unless otherwise noted, all Scripture quotations are from the *King James Version* of the *Holy Bible*. Copyright © 1982 by Thomas Nelson, Inc. Used by permission.
All rights reserved.

7710-T Cherry Park Dr, Ste 224
Houston, TX 77095
http://WorldwidePublishingGroup.com

Printed in the United States of America

Ebook: 978-3-9602-8433-8
Paperback: 978-1-365-80896-8
Hardcover: 978-1-60796-962-4

Table of Contents

Acknowledgements 11

Foreword 13

Introduction 15

Chapter One Having the Faith of God 17

    Faith is Foundational 19

    Faith for the Fight 20

    The Faith of Fathers 20

    Divine Connection 22

    Hearing God 24

    The Fruit of Faith 25

    Faith in Revelation 28

    Enduring Faith 29

    Living Faith 31

    Guided Faith 32

Chapter Two God's Place of Preparation is Hidden by Design 35

    Why Does God Hide Us? 36

    God Leads Us into Hiding 38

    God Commands a Blessing in Hiding 41

How Long will We be Hidden by God? 42

The Death of Progress 43

Hiding Develops Character 45

Intimacy Leads to Impartation 46

The Shrinking Reservoir 47

The Calling Out 49

Chapter Three The Worshipping Warrior 53

We are at War 57

Know Your Enemy 58

Know Your God 59

The Character of a Warrior 61

Discipline 62

Submission 65

The Place of Pressure 67

Obedience 68

Loyalty 73

Courage 74

Humility 74

The Last Word for Warriors 75

Chapter Four Developing Your Relationship 77

A Deeper Love 80

Bible Reading 82

The Lost Art of Meditation 83

The Jealous Lover 84

We are Doers of the Word 87

Obedience is the Divine Response 88

Chapter Five Divine Direction 93

What is Divine Direction? 94

The Purpose of Divine Direction 95

The Leading of the Lord 96

How do I Know When it is God? 98

The Ways He Leads 99

The Importance of Relationship 101

God, I Missed It. What Do I Do Now? 102

On the Right Path 104

Following His Lead 105

Chapter Six Positioned to Receive Instructions, Having an Ear to Hear 107

Another Revelation 108

How Do We Hear from God? 109

The Ways Which God Speaks 111

Dreams 111

Visions 111

The Prophetic 112

God Speaks Through Nature 114

Why Can't I Hear Him? 115

Positioning Ourselves to Hear 115

Do We All Hear His Voice the Same Way? 116

Recognition and Responsibility 117

The Proper Response 118

The Final Test.. 119

Chapter Seven There is an Expected End for You Purpose and Destiny
.... 121

Destiny and Purpose Working Together 122

Corporate Purpose 124

Fight.. 126

We Need Each Other 127

Understanding Who You are in the Lord.............................. 128

Fulfilling Destiny 130

Destiny and Purpose Work Together 132

Judas Iscariot- Son of Perdition 134

Jesus – Our Lord 136

Am I There Yet 138

Chapter Eight Is it Sin or Righteousness? 141

    The Struggle is Life... 142

    The Source of My Trouble 143

    The Darkness of God... 144

    The Darkness of the Enemy 147

    God's Judgment is on Sin.. 148

    Because of My Goodness 150

    God Forgives Sin 151

    The Grace of God.. 152

Chapter Nine Raising Your Level of Expectation, Times and Seasons 155

    What is Time?... 155

    The Search for Answers 157

    Discerning the Times 159

    You are an Eternal Being 161

    The God Spot 163

    Missing It 164

    The Right Place at the Right Time... 166

    Inventory 168

Chapter Ten The Finishing Anointing 171

    The Wayfarers 172

    It is time to Rule... 174

The Journey 176

When Will I Finish? 177

Identifying My Gifts 177

Renewed Vision 180

Kairos 180

Deliberate Success 181

Know Your Anointing 182

Acknowledgements

I would like to give special thanks and appreciation to all those whom I am indebted for the production of this book. There are so many individuals who have invested in me and through our relationship have pulled the best out of me. Thanks to the Almighty God, for His inspiration, guidance, and Holy Spirit poured on me day and night. I could not accomplish anything without Him.

I would like to acknowledge and thank my Life Center Church Pastoral Staff, Pastor Anetria Wright, MA (Executive Pastor and NBA Chaplain since 2001), Prophet Ron Wright, MBA (Assistant Pastor, Assistant NBA Chaplain and Finance Director since 2001), Dr. Veronica Williams - Latnie, PhD (Staff Clinical Psychologist), Pastor James Moss (Worship Pastor, International Recording Artist and Branding Specialist), Pastor Melanie Moss, MA (Marketing Specialist), Pastor Starlette Joyce, BA (Youth Pastor), Pastor Anita Hopes (Women's Ministry and Conference Coordinator).

To my Support Staff, Minister Ethel, Carol Wasnich, Minister Danai Makeleni, Deacon Calvin Burnett, Katie Green, and Minister Chris Alexander. To my Production Team, Nazir Ali (Media Specialist), Myles Wright, and James Moss Jr. To my Life Center Church Family and Friends, thanks for your labor of love and faithfulness.

Special thanks to Elder Melvin D. Latnie, who has had a long distinguished career in business and senior leadership positions at Michigan State University. Thank you for believing in me and investing in the production of this book.

Thank you Ms. Tamie Moran, Seline Nichols, Ms. Maleeka Love, Ms. Davida McShan, and Ms. Shawna Smith, with ENW Consultants for your assistance in editing this book for publication.

A deeply appreciate Elesia Powell for assisting in the early development of this book.

I especially grateful for my Spiritual Father and Covering, The Honorable Dr. Bishop Bill Hamon and the late Mom Hamon of Christian International. Your Anointing and Prophetic experiences has enhanced and inspired me. Thanks for your teaching and covering; it has maximized my potential and made an incredible influence on my life.

Also, special thanks to REJoyce Ministries Network and National Apostolic Prophetic School, of which have connected me with wonderful men and women of God.

As Senior Chaplain to The Detroit Pistons (22 years), I would like to thank Chauncey Billups, Grant Hill, Lindsay Hunter, Ben Wallace, Tayshaun Prince, Rodney Stuckey and The Detroit Pistons Organization.

To all the people who have been a blessing to me whose names were not mentioned, thank you for all you do to bless the Kingdom.

Sincerely,
Bishop Robert E. Joyce Sr.

Foreword

It is one thing to write a book which is not only intelligently well written, but also, comprehensive. This book is not only practical, but foundational, in that many of us have never truly understood the cohesive everyday events which challenge our Christian faith to the core. Challenges leaving many of us wanting and shaken. I believe manuscripts such as this, holds the mysteries to which will unlock those doors we've been kicking against, when it appears God does not answer our prayers, when it looks like the brook has dried up.

The two differentials of darkness are brilliant adaptations of Heaven and Earth. When one simply cannot determine whether it's God's darkness or the enemy's darkness, and for the commission to connect heaven to earth, we must be led by assignment and not emotion. Good work Bishop in explaining the two and giving us a road map for which to follow to victory when our brooks appear to have dried up.

Reading this book has empowered me to empower others. If you are looking for practicality, not religion, then this is your book. Real biblical answers for very real earthly challenges. Thank you Bishop Joyce for giving us this timely gift as we enter into a new level of Kingdom Empowerment!

Prophetess Dianne Palmer

Introduction

This book will encourage those who have been steadfast in their walk with God, but are discouraged because of their present trials. We often attribute our situation to the work of the enemy, but there are two types of darkness: the darkness of God and the darkness of the enemy. God will allow some God-ordained trouble to shape our lives. We can look at the lives of Moses, Elijah, and Jesus, recognizing times of darkness that were aligned with the will of God.

You are in the right place, at the right time! You are on course and God is still with you. Right now you may be in a dry place, like Elijah at the brook Cherith. Hold your position until you hear from God. This book will examine the commonality of adversity, while providing you with the keys to overcome it. We have all experienced setbacks, disappointments, the death of a dream, or the loss of a loved one. No matter what the difficulty has been (spiritual, relational, or economic) know that God's resources are available for you. He allows our circumstances to both deliver and develop us. Our current position is no surprise to God and He desires our very best. He says, "For I know the thoughts that I think toward you, saith the Lord, thoughts of peace and not of evil, to give you an expected end (Jeremiah 29:11, KJV)."

We will examine the life of the prophet Elijah. We can see that while God had Elijah hidden by the brook Cherith, he learned of God's provision and prepared for the toughest battle of his life; facing the prophets of Baal.

Today, God is calling us, His army, to be equipped for battle. This book will take you to boot camp where you will understand that soldiers are to be moved by assignment, not by emotion. You will learn how to get up after you have taken a hit. You will learn that you are a soldier, whose will, flesh, and character is under subjection to the will of the Father. And you will learn that God is developing your integrity and character by the brook because He wants you to look like Him.

Chapter One
Having the Faith of God

While sitting outside of a mall one summer day, soaking-up the sun and people watching, I noticed a young boy about seven years old with his dad. The child walked along the edge of a small stone wall. As his father warned him to be careful, the boy continued to walk toward the end of the wall and said, "Oh daddy, it will be alright. If I fall, you will be here to catch me." The boy reached the end of the wall and his father held out his hands as the little boy leaped into his arms. The child had faith that his daddy was able to catch him.

Understanding the trust the child had in his father was a powerful moment for me. It made me think of our relationship with God and how much He loves us. He always knows and desires the best for his children. God is always faithful, and because of his faithfulness we can put our trust in Him. The eternal creator, God, loves us and what is more remarkable is we did not do anything to deserve or earn it. He does not love you because you are good but because He is good. It is precisely because of His goodness that we can trust and have faith in Him.

We hear a great deal about faith, but what exactly is faith? How do we define something as intangible as faith? We can start by saying faith is a confident belief in the truth, value, or trustworthiness of a person, idea, or thing. Just like the little boy at the mall who had faith in his dad because he trusted him. The little boy had a relationship with his father and because of their relationship he had a confident belief in the trustworthiness of his dad.

Our relationship with God is similar. We trust Him based on our previous interactions and experience with Him. Jesus said, "If you, though you are evil, know how to give good gifts to your children, how much more will your Father in heaven give good gifts to those who ask him (Matthew 7:11 KJV)." If our natural fathers treat us well and care for us, how much more will the God of all righteousness hold our best interest near and dear to Him? He wants the best for us but our present circumstances may prevent us from seeing that our final outcome will be better. It is only through faith that we can remain steadfast and trust in His awesome ability to show Himself strong on our behalf.

Scripture tells us that, "faith is the substance of things hoped for, the evidence of things not seen(Hebrews 11:1 KJV)." As we have said, it is a belief in the intangible and confidence that the One who promised is faithful. What is our hope? The child at the mall hoped to scale the wall and since his father placed him on that wall, he believed it was possible for him to balance all of the way to the end of it. You may be in the middle of some unpleasant situations right now, but do not faint. The God that promised is faithful.

Faith is steadfast trust, which means I believe in you. Who or what are we to have steadfast trust in? Like the prophet Elijah, we have to put our trust in the true and living God to obtain the results we desire. God is not a manifestation of the mind of man but man is a manifestation of the mind of God. In addition, the scriptures are the revelation of the mind of God. Most importantly, we are the sons of God through faith in Christ Jesus (John 1:12).

Faith is Foundational

Faith is important because it is the foundation of Christian life. Faith is our initial deposit to God. If I am unworthy, what can I give a righteous God? We are righteous because of Jesus, but that is after we have received God's grace through faith. "Those who come to God must believe that He is and that He is a rewarder of those who diligently seek Him (Hebrew 11:6)." God extends His grace and He activates our faith by His love, then and only then can we truly worship Him.

Faith and worship are all we can offer a God who has everything at His command. We can believe His word and recognize His ability in all things. We cannot become believers until we accept the Gospel by faith. We must hear the Gospel and believe it in order to receive it (Romans 10:14-15). The principles of faith can be accessed by anyone who believes them. One of those foundational truths of Christianity is the principle of seed time and harvest. However, you do not have to be a Christian to reap the benefits of this principle; you only have to have faith in its operation.

Faith for the Fight

There are many books on faith and adversity. They teach us how to stand on the work and overcome life's difficulties. Our goal is not simply to hold on for dear life while the enemy whips us into near submission. We learn the art to war more skillfully with each battle, not only how to defend ourselves, but how to wage war. If we lose our faith, we will lose every battle that opposes us. Faith still comes by hearing the word of God for successful warriors. As our hearing increases, our faith advances, until our faith becomes like the faith of God. The faith of God speaks a word and the word that is spoken is established in the Earth.

Our faith has to be attached to the Word of God. It must be attached to God in order for it to be effective. Often people get into place where they have faith in faith, but this is not wise. We are to have faith in God alone and nothing else (Mark 11:22). Sometimes God allows the brook to dry up because we are guilty of trusting in it more than we trust Him. He wants us to be willing to follow where He leads, so He will sometimes dry up the brook to get our attention.

The Faith of Fathers

We really cannot discuss faith without mentioning Abraham. The scripture refers to Abraham as 'the father of faith' and that Abraham's belief in God was counted unto him as righteousness (Hebrews 11:7). Abraham believed God to provide a sacrifice on his way to Mount Moriah. As he began to climb the mountain with Isaac, Abraham told his servants that he and the boy would return. I would be remiss if I did not mention Noah. Noah faithfully preached for 400 years! Yet he was only able to save his own family from the flood. How foolish he must have looked building a boat on dry land. That's extreme faith – pushed to its' limits!

We can look at the experience of another of God's mighty servants, Elijah the Tishbite. The name Elijah means "the Lord is my God", and it represents the conviction of his life. He was loyal, devoted to God and was unwavering in his faith when facing opposition. He confronted Ahab and said, "as the Lord God of Israel liveth, before whom I stand, there shall not be dew nor rain this years but according to my word(1 Kings 17:1)."

When Elijah, who as of the inhabitants of Gilead, spoke of "the Lord God of Israel, before whom I stand", he was saying that he was in a constant relationship with the Lord. That is why I say we don't have to get anointed, we are always anointed. We should get away from this idea of a temporary anointing. We are always in covenant with God; therefore His anointing is always present. Sometimes we may have a more powerful manifestation of His presence than at other times, but because of our covenant we are not waiting for the anointing. We have the anointed Christ within us at all times (2 Corinthians 1:21 & 1 John 2:20).

A good example of this is marriage. There may be times when you feel more married than at other times, but you are always married whether you feel it or not. Consequentially, there is never a time we are not divinely connected with God. We are in covenant with Him and our covenant gives us authority and access to His power just as it did with the many mighty men and women of God before us. Therefore, we only need to have faith in God and His ability in us.

Someone may say, "Woo, I feel the anointing, or the anointing just came in." This is an inaccurate statement. Every time you see me whether you know it or not I'm anointed. This is a fact, but because of certain teachings, we get the idea – and it sounds good when we say, "I feel my anointing, or I feel my help coming." It may feel good to say, but the reality is that you are always anointed. I can tell you one fellow who knows that you are always anointed and that is that old slew foot devil. The devil knows that you are always anointed.

Divine Connection

Elijah made a declaration: he said, "I stand in the presence of God (1 Kings 17:1)." That's why he was not intimidated to talk for God because he had that interaction with God. We know the Old Testament tabernacle and temple had the Outer Court, the Inner Court, and the most Holy Place. Elijah is saying here; I do not hang out in the Outer Court. Before you were saved, did you ever go to a club and notice the folks who just hung outside near the door? They didn't really want to get involved. Well, there are some Christians who are like that, people who don't want to get truly involved in the church. They want to know God but have no desire to live in close relationship with Him. However, there are others who really want a relationship with God.

Then Elijah said, "…there shall not be dew or rain these years according to my word (1 Kings 17:1)." The prophet stands, in the presence of God, and comes to a place where he understands the ways of God. He understands how God thinks. Have you ever had somebody who knows how you think, who understands your pattern of thinking and who thinks like you? When they are around you, you can almost finish each other's sentences because you know each other so well. Now, that's relationship!

As a prophet of God I often hear someone say, "thus saith the Lord," to imply they are hearing from God. I know they are not telling the truth when they open their mouths because my God doesn't talk or act that way. Their words don't line up with the Bible. It isn't in the word. Our discernment of the sound of truth stems from our relationship with God. Paul says, I dare not go beyond my measure of rule, or his measure of authority (2 Corinthians 10:13-14). We also have authority over sickness and again that is birthed out of relationship. So, Elijah begins to release the power of God. He begins to say that nothing is going to happen other than according to my word.

In fifteen years, our annual prophetic conference was never snowed out. This is because we believe we have the authority to speak to the weather. There is an authority we have discovered out of the relationship with God and we speak to the elements. Not everyone can claim this. I know of a lot of conferences that get snowed out all of the time.

Hearing God

Elijah said, "And the Word of the Lord came to me" because he had a relationship with God. He could interact with and speak to God. Elijah could speak the mind of God. He understands how God feels about situations and circumstances. Then there comes a special word here, which was "and the word of the Lord came to him saying, Get thee hence." God told Elijah to get out of there. Elijah received new direction and he said, "...turn eastward and go and hide thyself (1 Kings 17:3)." God said, "I want you to hide yourself by the brook Cherith, that is before Jordan and it shall be, that thou shalt drink of the brook; and I have commanded the ravens to feed you there (1 Kings 17:5)." Elijah heard the word and obeyed it. He went and dwelt by the brook Cherith, which is before Jordan and the ravens did what they were supposed to do; they fed him!

Please notice that when the man of God did what he was supposed to, every other element did what it was supposed to do. The brook was doing what it was supposed to do. The birds were doing what they were supposed to do. The ravens brought Elijah bread and flesh in the morning and bread and flesh in the evening. Elijah's meals were provided and he drank of the brook. There is a time when God will do everything for you, won't He? All you have to do is sit, eat, and position yourself to receive from God.

There is something very interesting here, the scripture says, that it came to pass after a while the brook dried up. The prophet could have said "what in the world is going on here? I am where God has told me to be. I am doing what God has told me to do. I am standing in the presence of God and all of sudden the brook dries up?" Sometimes the sovereignty of God will give you an explanation for the things He does and other times He will not. This is a faith walk and your faith will be required when you don't understand why God is doing something.

Elijah understood the power of his faith. He understood the operation of his words in framing his world and he made a bold declaration that there would be no rain. This was based on his covenant and interaction with God. This is the same mighty warrior who slew 450 false prophets at one time because he had the faith of God. Have you taken anything for the Kingdom lately? Let's see how we can become skillful and precise warriors; and conquer for the Kingdom.

The Fruit of Faith

It is impossible to please God without faith (Hebrews 11:6). Our faith has to be active. It requires a corresponding action. Elijah had the faith of God. He was an example of his

Father-God because he was made in His image and likeness. He was given dominion. God gives us an idea of what we, through our God-kind-of-faith, can create with our words. We know this because he spoke a drought into existence and he did not doubt that his word would come to pass.

What did God's Faith look like? He believed His own words. God can't lie and whatever He says becomes tangible. The scripture reminds us that God created the heavens and the earth. Genesis 1:1-29 gives us a detailed explanation of how that took place. What we can see from the reference is that God spoke and whatever he spoke came into being. In total, it refers to God speaking at least nine times as He created the heavens and the earth. We know that God framed the worlds with His words (Hebrews 11:3). That is what the faith of God looks like. It is active and certain of its success. You have to say it before you can see it (Romans 4:17).

You may be wondering why the manifestation faith and yield of the faith are different in the lives of God's people and you may also be wondering are there different levels of faith in God? The answer is yes! The difference in our levels of faith has to do with how much of the word is applied in our lives. How much of what we have heard do we actually use? It would be like having someone come over to your house and show you how to use a telephone. You say "Okay, good", but once they leave, you take the bus across town to get in touch with them or go outside and yell down the street to reach them. If you would only pick up the phone and tap into the knowledge you have been given, your faith will grow as you use it.

Our levels of faith are directly related to our experiences. When we look at the life of David, we can see how he grew in his ability as a warrior. His first fight was with a lion and then he encountered a bear. It was because of those experiences that he was not fazed when his ultimate physical battle presented itself. The great Goliath was just another soldier in David's eyes. David was not frozen in fear like the armies of Israel. He was anxious to defeat Goliath and encourage the nation. David believed in the success of his outcome. David knew he would defeat Goliath and he said that God would deliver him out of his hand.

Elijah was confident in his relationship with God and he understood his authority to operate in God's stead. You may have the gift of faith, which is your ability to believe for something. As we have said, some may have faith in faith. We see this knowledge in programs the world has to offers such as the power of positive thinking programs. However, our faith is in the true and living God because the God-kind-of-faith is more than positive thinking. For the believer, faith is an operation of the heart (Romans 10:10). God imparts faith into your heart. The initial deposit is saving faith, as every man is given the measure of faith.

You may think, well I've tried that. I have said what I wanted and nothing happened. However, you must remember belief is only one of the components of faith. Do you truly believe what you are saying or are your words spoken from a fearful heart? If faith works by love, then increase your measure of love for the things of God. If we simply enjoy the presence of the Lord, He will give us our deepest desires. God can also help our unbelief through prayer, as He did in Mark 9 or Galatians 5:6. We must remember that God is sovereign and we should ask according to His will.

Faith in Revelation

Now, it looks as if Elijah spoke to the atmosphere and the brook dried up. In our minds we reason, all I have to do is speak to the atmosphere again and override the current issue. This is not accurate. The scripture says that the prophet cannot go beyond the Word of the Lord. Jesus said He did things to please the Father. How can we decide what the will of God is? In general, His will is His word; nonetheless individually His will is revealed by the Holy Spirit. There are times when God tells me everything about a situation and at other times He doesn't. That is just the way God operates. The brook dried up at Elijah's word. The question remains, what do we do when the brook dries up?

We live in the information age. Information is useful, valuable and necessary but revelation uncovers the hidden story or the backstory (1 Corinthians 2:9-11). God imparts revelation to us through our hearts. Information is received by our minds and can lead to human reasoning. God knows us and any man who loves God can rest in the knowledge that God knows him. Since He knows us, He knows what

His will is concerning us and He desires that we know His will also.

Enduring Faith

How do I know I am in His will, you ask? For far too long we have been under the misguided impression that being in God's will is always a place of comfort and calmness. We have heard when you are "in His will" there will be peace; a true statement. However, the peace we experience in God's will is not necessarily calmness but rather a certainty or assurance of our course of action. Elijah was in the will of God by the brook Cherith but because of the words He had spoken, the brook, which had sustained him, dried-up.

We could go on to mention Abraham, Moses, Job and others who serve to remind us that we can be in difficult situations and still be in the will of God. Of course, the most obvious example of this is our Lord. Jesus was perfectly centered in the will of God while He was on the cross. What He was going through was such a painful, degrading situation that He prayed more than once for an alternate outcome but resigned Himself to the will of God.

We must also develop enduring faith. We need faith that believes, gives its allegiance to, and puts credence in the will of God for our lives regardless of the current circumstances. There are times when our situations don't look as God said they would look. Things are difficult and they appear to be getting worse. Enduring faith understands that God is still who He says He is, and His work alone brings change.

Being assured of our course and standing in difficult situations is a true indicator of our faith. "As Christ suffered in the flesh, arm yourselves likewise (1 Peter 4:1)." Can we obey God when we are in a storm? When things don't look as you thought they would, will you still believe things will work out if we trust in God? We have to remember that "the just shall live by his faith (Habakkuk 2:4)."

It is through faith, praise, and wisdom, that we achieve dominion. When we have faith in God Himself, not merely faith in the operation of faith, it represents the God-kind-of-faith. It is because of our faith in God that we can praise Him in the midst of our battles. In fact, we must praise Him although we may be in a quandary. How can we repay God for all His benefits?

We can offer Him praise out of hearts. Our praise is not contingent on what God does but it is totally committed to Him for who He is. As we are standing in faith and offering God the sincerest praises of our heats, we must also apply the wisdom of God to our circumstances. Knowledge is the information and revelation we have obtained for our benefit. Wisdom is knowledge applied and we could write an entire book on that topic.

Living Faith

We have all seen faith in operation in history, by people who were not even Christians. I think about Mahatma Gandhi, who did not even believe in Jesus but had the faith to believe he could change a nation through nonviolent resistance. Gandi was so successful that his ideas were later incorporated into the civil rights movement led by Dr. Martin Luther King Jr. in the 1960s. We all know of the stores of the local people and the Freedom Riders who stood their ground against water hoses, vicious dogs, and bullets to change a nation. They called national attention to the disregard for the federal law and local violence used to enforce segregation in the southern United States. Police arrested riders for trespassing, unlawful assembly, and violating state and local Jim Crow laws, along with other alleged offenses, but they often first let white mobs attack them without intervention. Their enduring faith led them to stand, in spite of the current circumstances. Clearly this was a situation when things were not only difficult but rapidly getting worse.

Likewise, Rahab was a woman of extraordinary faith in the scriptures. Rahab was a Canaanite and a harlot, a woman of less than stellar reputation. It was because of her background that she was such an example of the power of faith. She was not an Israelite and was not familiar with their customs and moral standards. She had no knowledge of their historical background but she said that she knew the Lord had given them the land. She had heard of the Israelites conquest of the people all around Canaan and of how their God dried the Red sea. She declared by her word that the God of Joshua is, "the Lord your God, He is God in heaven above and in the earth beneath (Joshua 2:11)." Because of her faith, her entire household was saved from destruction. God has many, many treasures available to us. We only need to believe to receive our natural and spiritual inheritance.

If we have childlike faith, we will see the glory of God in our lives. When we are childlike, we will rest with the assurance that God has our best interest at heart because He knows what is best for us. We will operate like God, by speaking words of faith and allowing the plan of God to manifest. God will keep His promises. Over time, we will become certain that God is a promise keeper. We will encounter more difficult and seemingly impossible situations and watch as God delivers and works all things in our favor.

Guided Faith

I can remember going to look at my first house. I prayed that God would give me the house I wanted but I also prayed for His will to be done. I was already pre-approved for a mortgage but I did not want a house that was not mine. I knew that my prayer was strong enough to get the house, even if it wasn't God's best for me. How is that possible you ask? We all know of a time when we just wanted something so badly, that we begged God for it. We spoke the words of faith and believed God for it and He gave it to us.

Usually, it is not long after we get it that we wish we could send it back. I wanted the house God had for me, not just any house. I knew if God gave it to me, it would be impossible for anyone or anything to come against me in that house. I walked around the grounds and circled the house praying. I am certain the neighbors thought I was a little crazy but that didn't matter to me. God's will for me was my concern. I can honestly say all of my days in that house were blessed. Why, because I was in the will of God. It is important as a people of faith; we always seek the will of God concerning the issues we believe Him for. That way, we do not place ourselves in the position of asking for things to simply heap upon our flesh.

The believer's life depends on his walk of faith. The realities of life, with its dark places, disappointments and tragedies, will drain the strength out of you if you are not grounded in faith. God allows us to have a measure of faith and that faith operates by the love of God in our hearts. The scripture tells us that these three remain: faith, hope and love. The greatest of these is love (1 Corinthians 13:13). It is only our love for God and others that will enable us to continue to have faith throughout difficult circumstances. Today many say the evidence of their strong faith can be witnessed by their success, but what happens to them when they can no longer see the success they once had?

Points to Remember:

- *Faith is present and active*
- *Faith has corresponding action*
- *We encourage faith through relationship with God*
- *Our faith stirs us to advance the Kingdom of God*
- *We must say it, before we see it*
- *Faith is our foundation*
- *We must acknowledge God's ability in all things*

Chapter Two
God's Place of Preparation is Hidden by Design

The Count of Monte Cristo is a novel written by Alexander Dumas. In it Edmond Dantès, the protagonist, is nineteen when he is sent to prison by his enemies for a crime that he did not commit. While in prison as a political prisoner, he learns history, philosophy, languages and the sciences under the tutelage of Abbé's Faria. When the Abbé's dies he leaves Dantès a map to a fortune in treasure. Edmond Dantès escapes from prison in the Abbé's coffin and retrieves his fortune. The treasure is hidden on the Island of Monte Cristo. He uses the money to exact revenge on all of his enemies. He has been hidden away for years and none of his detractors recognize him, as he returns methodically to bring each of them to ruin.

    This story reminds me of what it is like to be hidden by God; like Edmond Dantès, we are typically in plain sight; but no one is able to see us for who and what we truly are until the appointed time. When we are hidden by God, we are being molded by God. Eventually we will be catapulted into destiny and take our enemy, the adversary, to ruins.

Why Does God Hide Us?

Being hidden by God can be like walking into a room and searching for a particular item. After being unable to find it, you walk away only to come back later and find the very item you were looking for was right in front of you the entire time. This can be frustrating and we wonder why we couldn't see the item the first time. Were we distracted, or maybe it was not in our line of sight?

While Jesus performed a couple of miracles up to age twelve, scripture reminds us that Jesus was hidden most of His life. During the miracle of preaching in front of the Pharisees and the Sadducees, we discover that it is the only time in the entire Bible where both of them are seated together at the Temple of God and they are listening to Jesus. After that time, we don't hear about Jesus any more until He is thirty years old. He was hidden for many years and He was noticed for three and a half years. Jesus, the Son of the Most High God was hidden for years, so what about you? Are you hidden by God?

In hiding, God builds us up and develops our character. At the same moment, He is concealing us from everyone else, God begins to show, unveil, reveal and manifest Himself to you. During this time He develops an intimate relationship with you all while allowing you to discover who He is and can be in your life. We learn to trust Him in hiding and He shows us that He trusts us to carry out His will. So when you finally come out into the forefront, you are in fit condition for immediate action and use. God is developing us into men and women of integrity. He is developing your gifts; and cultivating faithful stewardship.

God seems to hide us in clear view until He is ready for us to be revealed for His purposes. We can be destined, yet hidden until the specified or set time of God. As was said, even Christ was hidden in God until the time when He should be revealed (Galatians 4:4). Christ was foreordained before the foundation of the world but was manifest in time (1 Peter 1:20). It appears that times of being hidden and in wilderness experiences are all a part of the challenges for those who are destined, like you, and for those who want to do exceptional things for the kingdom.

What kind of place is the hiding place? It is desolate, solitary, and barren. Yes, God does provide for us during these times but the provision is just enough to ensure our dependence on His divine intervention. It is not an easy time, but the confidence that we are in God's will gives us the grace to go through the process. The hidden place is for your making; it is for your anointing. God hides us to prepare us to reign and have dominion so that we can begin to manifest the majesty of God from the inside out. When we begin to reflect His glory, then we know that we are being transformed into the image of His beloved son. Now that is success!

God Leads Us into Hiding

Powerful lessons can be learned in the hidden places. When we are alone with God that is when God will begin to show us His mysteries. There are many examples in scripture of those who were led into hiding by God. There are different types of hiding or wilderness experiences. Moses was exiled in the land of Midian for forty years. He was being prepared for the work of the ministry. The Israelites went through the wilderness, complaining all the way and they are a perfect example of what we should not do while we are hidden by God. The fish devoured Jonah for three days and nights and when Jonah came out he was ready for the work that God called him to fulfill. Elijah was sent to the middle of nowhere to hide. The lesson is that God wants us to come to a place where we are found faithful in our hidden life.

Isaiah was hidden until Uzziah died. How was Isaiah hidden? He was already a prophet, but Isaiah was so distracted by his love for King Uzziah that he was unable to see God clearly until after the king's death. Isaiah says, "in the year that King Uzziah died, I saw also the Lord" I believe he saw the Lord but he also saw himself in another light. We become authentic while in hiding, as the invisible becomes visible. Our focus becomes singular and as our vision of God becomes clear our self-perception is crystallized and defined (2 Corinthians. 3:18). If God holds the only true definition of my authentic self, then it goes without saying that I would have to have a clear vision of God in order to see myself. Many times we are still holding on to things that have become distractions and they are preventing us from seeing ourselves. Isaiah saw God and he received his specific commission. He was called before but now he was commissioned.

We all need to understand the importance of the hidden life. We need to know that there is value when God takes you, and puts you on the back burner for a while. He takes you out of the limelight and we don't like it when God holds us back. Before God will use us for His own glory, we must first pass by the brook Cherith, just as Elijah. Before God uses us, He takes us into hiding, He takes us into isolation. He has to have us alone with Him. Notice what the Father did with Jesus. In Luke 4:18, Jesus had to defeat the enemy in private before He could defeat him in public. God will take you behind the scenes and allow you to defeat the enemy in private.

Scripture reminds us to pray in secret and we will be rewarded openly. During your alone time is when you develop your relationship with God. God takes you off the scene and He cultivates foundational things on the inside of you. We found out that when we have true public praise, it is because we have true private praise. Private victory precedes public victory. Uproot all the negative things that you interact with during the course of the day. If you preach an hour, you need to pray two hours. If you watch television three or four hours a night, you need to pray at least half an hour.

Remember, when true ministry occurs, virtue leaves your body because true ministry releases the life of God. When virtue is released it has to be replenished. If you don't get the virtue replaced, the next time someone touches you nothing will happen. Virtue can only be replenished through the word of God and prayer. This is what happens when true ministry occurs.

In the season and time when God hides us, He'll also break us down so that His image may be revealed in us. God wants to write on the tables of our hearts, subsequently, when we are pressed, what comes out of us will be God. That's why God is interested in breaking you because once you are broken it is then that you become more powerful than you've ever been. As the scripture teaches, "His strength is made perfect in our weakness (2 Corinthians12:9)." The moment that I am weak, I begin to ask for His help. However, when I'm strong in my own mind I don't ask for His help.

We often say, "I can do this, I can work this out", but when we get into difficult situations we call for help. We plead with God, "I can't see my way out of this. If you don't help me, I don't know what's going to happen to me today." God loves for us to depend on Him. That's why the psalmist says some men trust in horses and some in chariots; in other words, some of us trust in the arm of flesh but David said I will trust in the Lord. "I will acknowledge Him in all my ways and He will direct my path (Proverbs 3:6)."

God Commands a Blessing in Hiding

The word command is a very powerful word. It does not ask, it is not a request, it is a COMMAND. When God commands a blessing it is a specific provision for a particular purpose and assignment. We must remember that during seasons of hiding, God will provide for us. God fed the Israelites with manna and quail and with this provision they had all that they needed.

God commanded a blessing for the prophet Elijah as he hid himself by the brook. The brook was a source of refreshing, the brook was a source of bathing and cleansing. There is supernatural nourishment in the hidden places of God. There will be enough provision to accomplish the plans and purposes of God. What do you need? Is your need attached to the purpose of God; then rest assured the need will be fulfilled.

His place is always complete with His provisions. Scripture teaches us that God directed Elijah to hide himself by the brook Cherith (1 Kings 17:3). Elijah was sent into the middle of nowhere to hide. God's call is always accomplished by God's provision. Wherever God takes you, He's going to provide for you because it's His responsibility. He will never send you to places in life that He does not give you provision for all that you need. I don't care how difficult it is for you, His Grace is sufficient.

Notice that before the need arose, God had already had provision in place. Before Elijah needed it or before he knew that he needed it. When He formed the world, He made sure there was a little brook just for Elijah. He knew Elijah was going to need some fresh water, so He made that brook just for him. Never forget that God knows your needs and God has your provision. He'll move Heaven and earth to see that your needs are met. God will do whatever it takes to bless you because you are so special to Him. Whatever it takes, scripture says that you will not be forsaken and you won't have to beg. God will do what He needs to in order to get His Blessing to you. He will even bless a whole nation to get to you because you're just that special!

God had a blessing for Elijah. While we are hidden by God, He will provide for us and command a blessing to sustain us. Jesus spent forty days and nights in a desert after He was led into the wilderness by the Spirit. Jesus shows us how to respond to times of being hidden (Matthew 4:11). We survive in hiding by not living on bread alone but by the words of God. Even the apostle Paul spent thirteen years hidden and in training for ministry (Galatians 1 and 2).

How Long will We be Hidden by God?

The time we spend in hiding, or in whatever type of wilderness experience we are a part of, depends on us. Our response to the circumstances will have a direct effect on the length of our time in the process. Once we are found faithful, God will expand our sphere of influence and bring us out of hiding. When we learn to keep confidences, then God gives us a platform to influence people at a greater level. Often when we are hidden, we get discouraged and distracted and we talk with the wrong people. The Israelites took forty years to travel a journey that should have taken no more than forty days. Why? Because their response to the divine trial was to complain and instead of going forward they went backward.

Have you ever been in process with God? You started to move in the things of God and you could see your growth in ministry; then suddenly fear grips your heart. It is not fear of failure in God, but it is the fear of success. The fear of success has derailed many from advancing and manifesting the majesty of the kingdom of God. Instead of continuing to move forward, you deliberately do something that you know will take you to the opposite direction away from the things of God. This is self-sabotage! For example, you were keeping your commitment to prayer and Bible reading and then you decide all the extra effort is not necessary. This is self-sabotage!

Ministry is a great responsibility and the thought of it may give us pause but it should not hinder us from doing the will of God. Some have the idea that if we don't advance the kingdom of God the enemy will not attack us. This is far from the truth. Our adversary is relentless and methodical with ages of experience but thank God we have the Greater One on the inside us.

The Death of Progress

Pride will keep us in hiding. Can we say enough about pride? It is the death of all progress in the kingdom of

God. There are many examples set before us which admonish us against any desire for self-promotion. Scripture reminds us of the six, "I wills", which caused Lucifer, the son of the morning, to be thrown out of heaven (Isaiah 14:12-20). I have a test I take whenever I am concerned that I may be operating in pride. I examine how many times I refer to my own will and desire rather than God's will and His desire, regarding a particular situation. If I find I have left God out, I know pride is not far behind. Pride is really a kind of independence which determines that it does not need the guidance of God. It is self-willed and selfish.

A friend of mine had a situation recently which sheds some light on this dilemma. My friend has been an ordained elder in a particular denomination for several years. He relocated for his job and subsequently had to find a new church. He and his wife were led to join a church which was of a different denomination. They knew they were in the right place at the right time but they were not acknowledged as elders or ministers just brother and sister. It was as if they had not previously gone through all those years of dedication and commitment to ministry. Their new leader, who was not familiar with all of their gifts and abilities, seemed to ignore them.

My friend felt frustrated and humiliated many moments but he stayed the course because he knew that he was in God's will. He and his wife prayed and eventually things began to change. They became the assistant pastors of that church before the Lord called them to their own successful ministry. You see, if they had walked out during their time of being hidden, they would still be going around the same mountain.

A pilot I know who told me they would stack aircraft in the sky, one on top of another at various altitudes whenever there is weather or some other delay. They were placed in a holding pattern in the airspace near their intended airport, so they could have clearance to land whenever space became available. When we respond properly to being hidden by God, we will be released from every holding pattern that has hindered our progress. The moral of the story is that a proud attitude has the ability to keep us going in circles. Jesus made Himself of no reputation and laid down His glory to complete His assignment.

Hiding Develops Character

Your time in hiding is designed to humble you, to prove you, to know and define what is in your heart. Why would an all-knowing God need to find out what is in our hearts? God knows us completely; He knows our core. We are tried in hiding but He tries us to reveal our own hearts. We are never a surprise to God. In hiding, God is removing some of the unnecessary baggage we have acquired and He imparting the articles that will be important for our journey.

The wilderness is designed to build up our spiritual house. It removes division and brings singular focus. It prepares us as peculiar people, to be kings and priest unto our God. It is the place where He perfects us. God says after we have suffered awhile He will perfect us, establish, strengthen and settle us. In hiding, we learn to trust God and His operation in us. Our faith is challenged in the hiding. You are tried and tested and as you overcome, you develop tenacity and vision. While we are hidden, God is building our character. Many gifts are in operation before the wilderness. However, gifts without character usually end in disaster.

The scripture reminds us of Joseph whose character was honed in the pit, in Potiphar's house and in the prison. He sustained and provided for God's people. He was not a priest or a king but he was in ministry through business. His character was developed in his hidden times. He could have grown bitter, greedy and selfish because of his past but he didn't hold on to his betrayals and disappointments. He let them go and God made him second in command to the Pharaoh of that day. After Peter had denied Christ, the Lord did not give up on him. Once Peter was 'converted' the scripture says, Jesus confronted Peter with the question, "Do you love me?" Jesus told him to "feed my sheep", which Peter did wholeheartedly until he was martyred (John 21:17).

Intimacy Leads to Impartation

We become familiar with God's presence while we are in hiding. While we are in hiding, we will learn that nothing takes the place of our personal prayer time alone with the Lord. It is through prayer that our relationship with God blossoms and our ministry matures. God is always active in our lives but we must remain active with Him. In hiding, we will learn that prayer is not an emotional experience, nor is it an intellectual experience, although both aspects of our personality are involved. Prayer is a spiritual endeavor directed by the Holy Spirit (Romans 8:26-27).

When we are hidden, we will learn what it truly means to delight ourselves in the Lord. As we delight ourselves in Him and minister to the Lord, our ministry to Him will renew our strength. When we respond to the hidden place of God as Jesus did, by living on every word of the Lord and then we know that we will reap a reward in God's appointed time.

When we take personal time in hiding with God, He makes us into worshippers, prayer warriors and preachers and in doing so we manifest His glory. What does it mean to be blessed? The best definition I have found for the word is: happy, fortunate, prosperous and enviable. It is the result of walking in the knowledge and wisdom of the Lord. This will be our general condition when we obey what we know in the word.

The Shrinking Reservoir

The prophet Elijah looked at the brook Cherith and he must have said "God it looks as if this thing is getting smaller than it was before. It's not quite as high as it used to be." The prophet was sitting there watching the brook dry up. It was getting lower and lower. Can you imagine how Elijah must have felt as he watched that shrinking stream?

He watched the brook as it got narrower and narrower and then one day there was nothing left. It was dry. All the water has gone. In the current economy, we have seen this play out repeatedly.

The scripture advises us to "just shall live by faith," (Habakkuk. 2:4). The question remains, what do we do when our brook dries up? What are we going to do when we no longer have the resources that we once had? That job that we invested our lives in dries up, or the business we worked so hard to build no longer turns a profit.

I never will forget when I was working at General Motors. I thought I was going to retire from General Motors but I heard the voice of God say that it was going to begin to dry up. You have to understand that those of us who worked in the plant knew that some folks worked and lived off their overtime. They thought overtime was their standard income; they began to live their lives on it. When the economy started to go bad, the first thing the company cut back was overtime and it became hard for employees to live on a regular forty hours per week salary because they raised their standard of living to that of overtime salary.

God sometimes allows that job we have depended on to begin to dry up. Have you ever been working somewhere and when you first get there you love going and can't wait to get your lunch ready the day before because you like your job? Then you start going there and it begins getting harder to go. If you have ever had a job like that then you know that on Friday, you are thinking about getting out of there and are probably tired already just thinking about going to work on Monday. There is a shift that begins to happen and you know God is speaking to you about moving on from that particular place.

The Calling Out

The time will come when God calls us out of hiding. When it pleased God, He called you forth to His kingdom (Romans 8:30; 1 Peter. 2:9; and Galatians. 1). There is a calling out among God's people. When we became engrafted into the kingdom, we were called out by God. "Kaleo" is the Greek word for called. It is much like receiving an invitation or an appointment. It is a call like the sound of a trumpet blowing. We recognize the sound because God gives us the ability to hear.

Our initial call is to salvation. We are also called to be ministers of reconciliation. When we are called out of hiding, we are well equipped for our ministry assignment. When Moses came out of hiding, he confronted the most powerful ruler of the known world. When Elijah came out, he faced the prophets of Baal and made a mockery of them and their god. Once Jesus came out of the wilderness, He began to destroy the works of the enemy and He continues to do it today (1 John 3:8). When God calls us out of hiding, we are ready to face any conflict. We begin to hate what God hates and love what he loves.

The Apostle Paul spent ten years in hiding or training for ministry. He traveled through the desert of Arabia and went on to Damascus, Jerusalem and other cities. When he came out of hiding, he wrote most of the New Testament, established churches and preached the gospel. Paul counted all of his education and his pedigree as nothing when he compared it with what he refers to as the, 'excellence of the knowledge of Christ'. After his time in hiding, he was equipped for his assignment. Are you ready to move into your assignment?

My pilot friend also told me that during international flights, the aircraft nears a certain point after takeoff and the pilot calls back to the flight attendants in the cabin to ascertain the conditions in the aircraft. The cabin crew informs the captain if there are any problems on board. This would be the time to turn plane around before the aircraft gets further away from the mainland, therefore, not being able to land for several hours. The pilot calls back and simply says 'coast out,' which means that they have reached a point of no return. There is no land in sight, only miles of ocean beneath and the northern lights above. They have to go forward because the option of turning around would severely delay the flight. When we are released from hiding, we are in 'coast out' conditions. The past has lost its power to deprive you of your future! We are at the point of no return and we must press ahead in purpose.

When we emerge from hiding, we will have acquired the finishing anointing. This is what we have been waiting for. The finishing anointing gives us the supernatural grace to complete our assignment. It is a new level of operation, where we will have 'peitho' the Greek word for confidence.

We will be convinced and have an inward certainty and trust that we are able to do the greater works that the scripture calls us to.

Points to Remember:

- *We are hidden by design*
- *When we are hidden, we are being molded by God*
- *We are hidden to prepare us to reign and have dominion*
- *Our response to the circumstances will have a direct effect on our length of time in process*
- *Pride is the death of progress*
- *God will command a blessing for us*
- *The commanded blessing is a specific provision for the particular purpose and assignment*
- *God holds the only true definition of our authentic selves*
- *Hiding builds character*
- *When it pleases God will call you out of hiding*
- *God is always active in our lives*

Chapter Three
The Worshipping Warrior

"Know your enemy, know yourself,

and victory is never in doubt, not in a hundred battles "

Sun-tzu

The following excerpt is from "The Art of War" by Sun-tzu.

"Master Sun Wu was from the state of Qi. On account of his treatise on the Art of War he obtained an audience with He Lu, the king of Wu.

"I have carefully studied the thirteen chapters of your treatise," said the king. "Would it be possible for you to give me a small demonstration of the drilling of troops?"

"Certainly I can," replied Master Sun.

"Can this demonstration be performed with women?"

"It can."

The king authorized him to proceed. One hundred and eighty of His Majesty's most beautiful concubines were summoned from the inner apartments of the palace and Master Sun divided them into two companies, putting one of the king's favorites in command of each company. All of the women warriors were given a halberd to hold. Master Sun now addressed them.

"Can you tell your front from your back, your left hand from you right hand?"

"We can," replied the women.

"When I give the order 'eyes front!' you are to look forward," said Master Sun.

"When I command 'eyes left!' you are to look to the left. 'Eyes right!' look to the right; 'eyes rear!' look to the back. Is that understood?"

"Yes!" replied the women.

With these rules established, Master sun had the executioner's ax set up (to show that he meant business). He went through the commands again and explained them several times. Then he beat on the drum and gave the order to face to the right. The women all burst out laughing.

"If my orders were unclear," said Master Sun, "and not properly understood, then I, as your general, am to blame."

So he went through the commands once more, explaining them in detail. This time he beat out the order to face left. Once again, the ladies of the harem burst out laughing.

"While my orders were unclear and not properly understood, I as your general was to blame. But now, since my orders were clear and since you understood them properly, the fault lies with your commanding officers."

And he gave the order for the concubines placed in command of each company to be decapitated.

The king was watching all of this from his terrace. He was appalled by this order to behead the two concubines he loved most in his entire harem and dispatched one of his aides with the following command:

"His Majesty has already witnessed sufficient evidence of your ability as a general. Without these two concubines, His Majesty would lose his appetite. He therefore desires that the order for execution be rescinded."

"Please inform His Majesty," Replied Master Sun, "that as his personally appointed general, I have total authority in this matter. I am unable to obey certain of His Majesty's commands."

And so he proceeded to have the two concubine-commanders beheaded, as an example to the rest. The two concubines next in rank were now installed as the new company commanders. Once again Master Sun beat the drum. This time the ladies faced left, faced right, marched forward, marched backward, knelt, rose to their feet, all in the strictest conformity to Master Sun's commands and all in total silence. Afterward he submitted the following report to the king:

"Your Majesty's troops have now been correctly drilled and Your Majesty may inspect them. They will perform Your Majesty's every bidding. They will go through fire and flood for Your Majesty's sake."

"You may take a rest," said the king, "and return to your quarters. I have no desire to put them into practice."

With this, King He Lu knew Master Sun to be a capable commander and took him into his service as a general. To the west, he conquered the state of Chu, entering the city of Ying. To the north, he struck fear into the states of Qi and Jin and became renowned among the feudal lords. And Master Sun shared in the king's might."

We are at War

War is bloody and gruesome, unfortunately, there are always some casualties. Casualties in a spiritual sense are people who are deceived by the enemy and abort the plan of God for their lives. Casualties become snared in one of the traps of the enemy: the lust of the flesh, the lust of the eyes and the pride of life. I will not name those who have fallen prey to his devices to avoid adding insult to injury. But many who have started on the road of righteousness have fallen off the path. Even to the point of denying the God who saved them and they resort to preaching another gospel. How can this be you ask through the subtle deception of the enemy? Don't think too highly of yourself for not being caught in a snare. Have you prayed for those who are caught in a snare? The scripture reminds us to restore the fallen, meekly. It is a poor army that leaves its wounded on the battlefield.

We are in an army. The army is known as the army of the Lord. We are warriors for Christ but unlike natural wars, the spiritual battle was already won on Calvary over 2,000 years ago. All that is required of us is that we remain faithful to Jesus and enlarge His kingdom. It sounds easy; unfortunately, our enemy goes about as a roaring lion seeking whom he can devour. The fact that he seeks one to devour means that he is not able to devour everyone. There are some who are more vulnerable than others. To avoid his snare we must identify the enemy and spy out his tactics.

Know Your Enemy

The scripture admonishes us not to be ignorant of the enemy's devises. One of the great warriors of scripture was Samson but Samson became a casualty. His position was that of a Nazarene priest and he had certain requirements that were placed on his life from birth. He was a mighty man, an anointed warrior but he was never able to take his position seriously and maintain his focus. Like many of us, Samson had a problem. He had a weakness. He was distracted by his desires.

In the course of events, he lost his eyes and more importantly he lost his anointing. His anointing was most significant because spiritual things cannot be seen with physical eyes. When you are anointed, you can see in the spirit realm all that you need to know in the natural. Yes, he repented and accomplished his mission but with much trial and heartache which he could have avoided if he had maintained his position. In the end, he succeeded in defeating the Philistines and regaining his anointing.

Unlike man, the enemy of our souls is relentless and organized. His attacks are calculated to steal, kill and destroy. His desire is to have you in his kingdom. His kingdom is marked by pride, rebellion, arrogance, deceit, hatred, bitterness and self-assertion. He speaks lies and opposes truth. He wants to make you a messenger of hell. Your enemy wants to cause sickness in your mind and body. He'll tempt you to live according to your human knowledge and wisdom, totally independent of the knowledge of God.

He'll attempt to isolate you from loved ones by causing abandonment, betrayal and disappointment. He begins attacking us in our youth. Afterward, we become unable or unwilling to trust anyone fully, hindering our God-given destiny in Christ.

But most of all, our enemy wants to entrap us with pride (Prov. 16:18-19). Pride will cause us to deny the power of God, or make the mistake of claiming His power is our own. Many, who have passed the test of the flesh and have seen beyond the lusts of the eyes, were finally caught in the pride of life. Walking in the power of God is exhilarating but we must remember that everything we have has been given to us by God. Every gift in our possession was given by Christ. He led captivity captive and gave gifts unto men. He is in all things and before all things and by Him all things consist (Ps.2:1-2; Ezek. 16:40-50; Dan. 4:30; Rom.1:28-32; 2 Tim. 3:2; and Jude 16).

Know Your God

We come to know the Lord through intimate fellowship with him. I can never learn your ways if I don't spend any time with you. Our fellowship with the Lord is like the relationship between a husband and a wife. The scripture refers to the church as the bride of Christ and collectively we form the Church, the body of Christ.

The relationship between husband and wife is deeply intimate. The intimacy that is shared between the two has the ability to conceive life. We, as the bride of Christ, have the seed of righteousness within us and when that seed is watered by spending time in the presence of God it will germinate, or we will conceive and deliver according to the mind and will of God.

We are brides, yet we are children who were conceived in the mind of God through Christ by the Holy Spirit. He did it because he loves us. He is privy to the core of our being. He knows us, yet, he loves us. It is a love so powerful that it transforms us into sons of God. There is no deeper love than the love of Christ for his church and remember you are the church.

When we know God, we have the ability to accomplish our goals. Do you know him? When you know God, you realize that He is with you no matter what you are facing. In joy and in tears, in victory and in defeat, in life and in death, He will never leave you or forsake you because He loves you and He is your reward (He has your back). A warrior's belief must be solely tied to Christ. He cannot have any divided loyalties. He carries his cross for one commander. He falls in line for one master – Jesus. Believe in the Lord your God, so shall ye be established believe his prophets, so shall ye prosper (2 Chron.20:20).

The strength of the warrior is contingent on his ministering to the Lord, only then can he renew his strength and mount up with wings as an eagle. As the warrior spends time in intimate fellowship, his spirit will become dominant and he will acquire the ability to put his flesh under subjection. Walking in the spirit helps the warrior develop the character he needs to be an effective warrior.

The Character of a Warrior

What I have found most intriguing is that the character of the warrior and that of the worshipper share many traits. They must walk in the spirit so that they will not fulfill the lust of the flesh. They must be skilled in the use of their weapons. The traits of the worshipper and the warrior enhance one another, so that they coexist and fortify the worshipping-warrior. What is worship and how does it influence the warrior?

The word worship has its roots in the old English word worth-ship. Worth-ship is to esteem the significance of a person or thing; it suggests that you understand its true value. The worshipping warrior appreciates the worth of his or her relationship with the Lord. Worship replenishes the warrior. He cannot be effective in battle if he is not strong in his spirit. He must "be strong in the Lord and the power of His might" (Eph. 6:10). How many times did Jesus, our ultimate example of a worshipping warrior, find time to get away from the crowds and the disciples to spend time with the Father in prayer and worship?

A warrior must worship or he will find himself resorting to his flesh to resolve matters. A worshipper must be skilled in battle or he will be waiting to be rescued from every skirmish with the enemy. It is only in the spiritual realm that the warrior will find his weapons (2 Cor. 10:3-6).

His weapons are: Prayer and time would exhaust us to discuss the importance of prayer. The practice of prayer is found throughout the scriptures. In fact, the Lord says, that His house will be called a house of prayer and that men ought to pray always. I am certain that he would not tell us to pray, if it had no value.

In fact, the value of a solid prayer life is evidenced in the scriptures. The disciples prayed so effectively that their shadows healed the sick. What should you pray? Pray the word of God. In Ephesians chapter six, the warrior is dressed for battle. In his hands, he holds only one offensive weapon; the sword of the spirit which is the word of God. When you pray the word of God, you are waging war against the forces darkness. If you desire to wreak havoc on the enemy--pray.

Fasting is also a weapon. When we fast we bring our flesh under subjection to the will of God. Fasting makes us more sensitive to the spirit realm and places us in harmony with the kingdom of God. Prayer and fasting are two disciplines we should practice developing to acquire the character of a warrior.

Discipline

Someone said discipline without consequence is merely a suggestion. We're in boot camp. Anyone who has been in the military knows what boot camp is all about. In boot camp, we learn discipline. Along with discipline you will find accountability, in other words there will be repercussions for your actions. We must know, that we can't behave anyway we want to at any time without consequence. Boot camp is a time of training and mental and physical conditioning, where we learn to pay attention to details.

If you have never been in boot camp you don't understand those kinds of things but only those who have truly been can say that they know what boot camp is and what basic training is all about. They have an understanding. They have a mindset of what it takes to be in boot camp. They're in intensified training for a season and they come out of boot camp having learned, specifically, how to be a better solider. God has you in a juncture when the brook dries up and He is taking you immediately into boot camp.

I believe boot camp is a time when you actually get away from home. It's taking you out of your environment and taking your environment out of you! It's removing you from your comfort zone. It places you in a whole new environment which causes you to have to trust and learn a whole new system. It's fascinating, those individuals who do not learn discipline at home, will have to learn it elsewhere. You can learn it at church, on your job, in the military, or you can learn it in jail. God calls us an army.

There is a mindset that God is trying to develop in His people. Many times we see ourselves only as that bride. If you see yourself as a bride, there is a certain mentality that goes along with that. Brides are dainty and don't want to get their white dress dirty. You don't want to mess up your nails and hair. But it's a different mindset when you are in the army. The mindset of a marriage and the mindset of an army are two different mind sets.

When you are getting ready to get married, it's all about the bride. They get all that accolades, the camera is waiting on you, the preacher waits on you; everyone's waiting on you. The army isn't like that. You find out real fast what a full day of work is all about. In the army, they want you to work a full day. Not a part day, not a couple of minutes, with a break every fifteen minutes.

In a military setting, you are transformed from a wimp into a mighty warrior. If there were no enemy, then there would be no need for an army, nor there a need for warriors. Warriors are the elite fighters of an army. They are not your typical fighters. They are trained in special tactics; they practice using their weapons and fighting on a continuous basis. Warriors are the special forces of warfare. Regular fighting calls for the Army or the Navy but when there is something that needs to get done swiftly and quietly, they call for the Special Forces, Reconnaissance, or the Navy Seals. Some warriors are born fighters, but most are made in boot camps. Warriors have to make sacrifices because skill takes practice. You will never become proficient at something that you don't practice. Warriors don't lose their concentration; they are disciplined.

A friend of mine shared this story with me. He said that he wanted to do a powerful work for the Lord. He wanted to be a warrior. He went to church one day and there was a gas leak just before service. The sanctuary had a heavy odor from the fumes. The church dismissed to the parking lot to wait for the gas company to correct the problem.

My friend said that instead of wanting the leak to be fixed so they could have church, he wanted them to cancel service, so that he could go and have breakfast at his favorite restaurant. Once service resumed, my friend had difficulty getting back into the flow of worship. He was thoroughly distracted in the thirty minutes that he waited outside the building. He recognized how easily he was moved from the things of God.

It may appear to be a small thing that he lost his concentration and his focus but that is not characteristic of a warrior. Any lapse of concentration on the battlefield can be costly. What my friend needs is discipline. You did run well, who did hinder you? (Gal. 5:7). Have you been working at a reasonable pace and then suddenly stopped in midstream? It is a distraction from the enemy. The warrior must be tenacious. He or she must not be easily pulled apart from their assignment. They must develop discipline.

Submission

I tell people that submission has become a dirty word but the kingdom of God has a certain order. The people you submit to and honor will have a direct relation to your success. Submission is getting underneath the vision and purpose of another person and assisting to push them upward toward their goal. Submission does not necessarily mean total understanding or agreement. You may not understand every move that your leader makes but if you trust that they are a man or woman after God's heart, you should have little trouble trusting their decisions.

Well, how two can walk together unless they agree? The majority of the time you will be in agreement, if you are submitted. But there will be times when you don't happen to agree with an order that your leader gives. That doesn't mean that you can do whatever you want because you don't happen to agree with the current marching orders. There are things that a leader sees that you cannot see from your perspective. Like a well-trained solider, if you simply follow the orders you will benefit from your obedience (Heb. 13:7).

I am in no way suggesting that you check your mind at the door when choosing to follow a leader. There have been too many instances of people being abused by leaders who have disenfranchised themselves from the spirit of God by their own actions. The scripture reminds us to follow leaders as they follow Christ and we must be able to take direction.

When you fail to submit to Godly leadership, you will not profit spiritually from the relationship. You are essentially wasting your time. You will not take on their anointing. You will not grow in the grace and knowledge of our Lord Jesus Christ. Your branches will be barren and your tree will not bear fruit because the leader that the Lord has sent into your life is unable to prune your branches. Submit and grow!

The Place of Pressure

That's what church is all about. God is assigning you to a particular division of His military. So God looks up and says "okay, all right, I need you to be in this army over here at this location" but you have to see the big picture. When you go where God tells you to go and you understand the principle and can submit, you glean from the anointing of your leader. There are certain things that God is supposed to impart into you and He is good at imparting those things. That's why I can't be afraid when God moves individuals out and moves in other individuals. God's in charge.

Church is a place where you get transformed. It's a place where God puts you beside someone who will get on your NERVE. The Bible says as iron sharpens iron (Prov. 27:17). In God's training process, He'll put someone in your path who rubs you the wrong way. Iron sparks and it makes you better, but the sparks fly. What we have to do is learn to work through difficult situations. God will put you in a church where sooner or later you'll have conflict. It's still God. That's why you can't run from church to church because if it's God's lead, then the next church you go to He will still have the same test waiting for you. If you like to fight, He puts you beside someone who is also like that because He's working on you. God loves you too much to let you stay the same.

When you come into the army of God He reassures us that He will complete the work he starts in us. God says I'm going to get what I need into you one way or another. When you are assigned by God to a particular military camp or military school, the guy in charge imparts into you things that he thinks will make you to be a better soldier. It's a place where the men and the boys are separated. It's a place of pressure. Gethsemane means a place of pressure. God the Father said, I want my Son to represent Me well. I'm going to send Him to Gethsemane, the place of death and I'm going to squeeze the last little bit of His soul out of him. The last part of your soul is self-will.

When you get in the military, they break down your will so you move and function as one unit and not do your own thing. God says, ok you want to do your own thing; I have to take you to Gethsemane, place of death. I am not going to kill you but will make you wish you were dead. He squeezed Jesus to the point that the scripture says the blood vessels around his brain began to bust. In prayer Jesus finally said, is there another way? He said no, not My will but Thy will be done (Luke 22:42). You have to stop by Gethsemane. We had a church around here named Gethsemane. And they changed their name. It's not Gethsemane any more. I guess somebody got the revelation.

Obedience

Boot camp is a place where you learn about WAR. If you're not successful in boot camp, you'll never be successful on the battlefield. If you can't win a battle in the church, you'll never win a battle in the world. If you don't make it through boot camp, you're going to be a target out there and you're going to be singing, "I was wounded in the Army of the Lord." I just can't get along with church folk. Stop complaining and give me ten pushups.

In boot camp, you begin to know what's important and what's not. Your priorities change once you get to boot camp. Once the brook dries up your priorities change. You go from needing to have a Pepsi to being able to get anything to drink. In boot camp, you start out wanting the glass to be nice and clean. But after you have been thirsty awhile, you don't care if you use an old dirty glass and just rinse it out once. I'll drink out of it because I'm in boot camp. I need water. If I can't get a glass, I'll drink out of my hand. Oh, it can become extremely unpleasant.

I'm like Gideon's army. I'll get on my knees and drink the water because my priorities changed once I get into boot camp. You can tell who's in boot camp and who isn't. The whiners and complainers aren't in boot camp. It's a place where men and women lose their rebellion. I watch people. I tell the ushers, have the ones in the back to come to the front. I watch some of them say, "I sit wherever I want." You don't think I see that rebellious devil. I see it! I just praise the Lord. I'm going to call the devil out of you sooner or later. I'm just waiting until the right time. It's a rebellious nature that does not obey delegated authority and our job is to drive it out.

Obedience says, "Oh yes, I'll sit right here, where do you want me to sit because I'm in the army? I'm coming for training." Boot camp is a place where you learn to follow orders and follow leaders. You follow whoever the leader is. There are times when I'm the leader. There are times when the worship leader is the leader. There are times when the usher is the leader.

I go to churches sometimes and want to sit back on the back row. I'm there to support the ministry. I do what I'm told to do because I understand that I am in an army. I come as a preacher. For example, if there is no one to catch people falling, then I know it's time for me to help catch falling people. I take off my Bishop hat and I put on my catcher hat. I become a catcher because I'm in the army and if one falls we all fall. I'm obedient to the leader.

God says you have to first be faithful in another man's work before He gives you your own, so part of basic training is, submitting to authority. When you get your own, you'll have authority because you submitted to authority.

We defeat the devil behind the scenes before we defeat him publicly. Before we can have an impact on our local area, we have to have an impact inside the church. How are you going to drive out devils and you can't hold your hands up through a whole worship song? I tell you to pray for one hour and then we have twenty-four hour prayer and you have excuses why you can't pray. If you can't pray for one hour let us know, so we can get someone to take your spot. We don't want the gap in the fence. We don't want the devil to be able to slip in the fence.

Boot camp is a place where you are told what to do and you say "yes sir" to the command. You don't have a mind in boot camp. Commanders don't care about your opinion in boot camp. They don't want to know what the Lord has said to you. All they want you to do in boot camp is follow instructions. Let me say it another way for individuals who are soft spirited.

If God sends you to a place, then every word that He says will line up with the vision. It will be in harmony with the vision of that house. He did not tell individuals to come to a house and redirect the house. Correction from beneath is always rebellion. Your kid can't tell you what to do. That's rebellion. I never tell Bishop Hamon, my mentor, what to do. I have ideas and suggestions that he may or may not use if he desires and he listens to those that are truly from God. I understand submission to authority and God' wants us to recognize it. Once we submit to authority, He gives us more authority.

They were remodeling the area that I live in and while driving home, the police stopped me. All I wanted to do was simply go around the corner but they're directing me to go another way. The officer said, "No young man, you've got to go the other way." He placed his hand right on his holster and I fully understood what that meant. I'm so glad that I can understand English. I prayed in the Holy Ghost and did as I was directed. I went the other way. You don't have to pull out your authority with me. You don't have to enforce it. I believe you! It's the same with God. I believe Him. When He puts me in a place, I listen to Him because He knows what's He is doing.

The training, discipline and pressures that soldiers go through make them stronger and it matures them. So whatever you're going through, the purpose of the discipline is to make you a stronger soldier. God puts us through stuff because He's interested in making us better soldiers. The brook has dried up and it's not to kill you. It's not to destroy you. It is not because you are angry nor is it because God is angry with you. It isn't because you sinned. It's because He's interested in making you stronger. He's interested in maturing you.

There are some things you can only gain by going through the trial. You can't get better by simply reading a book. You don't get this by just watching and you don't get it in some easy chair. You get it by going through. But what the soldier does learn in a short time is essential to his survival on the battlefield. You get it by actual training. A soldier has to leave the comfort of his home. He has to be put in a place all alone where it's dry, where it's lonely, where it's personal.

That's what God does to us. He gets us to a place where it's all about you and God. While in boot camp, it looks as if you're misunderstood. Nobody ever understands me, you'll say. God wants you to Himself. God will pull people away because He wants you all alone. He is tired of you bringing Bill, Jan, Gary and Tyrone with you. Boot camp is a place where the military sends its soldiers and teaches them an immense amount within a short time. The information that the soldier learns in a short amount of time is essential for their survival in the battlefield. What you're going through is essential for your battlefield. God takes you to a place where you must totally depend on Him.

Loyalty

A worshipping warrior must be faithful to his cause. When we find something or someone worthy of our fidelity then we should make the commitment to stay on course until our assignment is complete. It is easy to be loyal when you understand your mission. Your destiny is tied to the place and the people where God has called you. If you move before the time, you will find that you are in a constant state of beginning again, yet never truly fulfilling your destiny and you will be constantly learning but never coming into the realization of the truth. Be faithful and you will begin to see the fruit of your labors.

When we are loyal, God will provide the resources we need to complete our assignment. Take inventory of the fruit your last assignment produced and ask yourself if God is pleased. Loyalty means holding your position through adversity. When God positions you, it will not always be comfortable. There will be times when you will need to be corrected. There will be times when you simply have to wait and waiting can be terribly uncomfortable. Just remember that you are conforming to the image of Christ while you wait. Dedicate your heart toward the cause you're fighting for and be loyal.

Courage

Courage is the moral strength to resist opposition. The warrior must be comfortable with uncertainty. The only thing that the warrior can be certain of is the immutability of the council of God. God does not change. The scripture says that He is always the same. We can be confident and take courage in the direction of the Lord once we are confident of His will.

The warrior may be fearful at times. Fear should not be ignored. Acknowledge it and let the Holy Spirit endow you with power to wage every battle you face. The leading of the Holy Spirit will warn us and allows us to know whether we should fight now or wait to pursue and overtake. We cannot be named with the fearful and the unbelieving. We have a faith fight and we must wage war in the heavens.

Humility

The scripture reminds us not to think more highly of ourselves than we ought. Humility is a modest opinion or estimate of one's own importance. Jesus made himself of no reputation and laid His glory aside to accomplish the will of the Father. When you are busy protecting your reputation you will be unable to have a radical effect on the world for the kingdom's sake. You are too preoccupied with what *they say*. You know - *they* - we are always talking about what *they* said but no one seems to know who *they* are. What God says, should be our utmost concern since we live to satisfy Him. God can use us mightily for His kingdom when we are humble. Humility is the opposite of pride. Yes, we should esteem ourselves but not in pride and arrogance. The world refers to it as self-esteem. I call it God esteem. This is when we allow the spirit of God to manifest the majesty of the Lord through our lives. So stay low in your own mind and humble yourselves under the mighty hand of God and in due season, He will exalt you (1Pet. 5:6).

The Last Word for Warriors

Lastly, we must always remember that warriors take the spoils. What are the spoils? Souls are the spoils. Deliverance for the oppressed is spoil. Healing is a spoil. Financial stability is a spoil. It means that we have to go to battle to get them. If there are no spoils, what is the purpose of the battle? The points we should remember are:

Points to Remember:
- *There is a spiritual war being waged*
- *We are soldiers in that war*
- *We cannot be ignorant of the enemy's devices*
- *Warriors need intimate fellowship with God*

- *Warriors must be skilled with their weapons*
- *Worship energizes the warriors*
- *The warrior must walk in the spirit to develop the character he requires*
- *Discipline, Submission, Obedience, Loyalty, Courage and Humility are the traits of a warrior*

Chapter Four
Developing Your Relationship

Two friends were warming by the fire having a discussion about church. One friend determined that it was not entirely necessary for a person to attend church because one could see all the information they needed about God from other sources. The next friend listened carefully and held his peace. He decided to prove his point without much conversation. He went over to the fireplace and took one of the coals off the stack and placed it on the hearth.

They sat and continued to talk for a long while and the next friend pointed out that while they were there talking the coal had lost all of its heat. He suggested that the coal represented the believer without a relationship to a body of believers in a local church; eventually the believer would grow cold and lose all of his fervor for the things of God (Charles Spurgeon).

Although, church attendance is only one aspect of our relationship with the Lord, it is a crucial element in our spiritual growth. One of the tricks of the enemy is to try to get you to look at TV, or go on the Internet and view a church service and not attend church in person. Let me tell you, neither of them takes the place of joining and being a part of the local assembly. It's the same old enemy with a new device that's all. He has a new twist to keep you at home. I can have church by myself you say. That's a lie of the enemy. We know that we are the church but we have to fellowship with others in order to have church and in order to fulfill the word of God (Heb. 10:25). The word of God requires us to be a part of that local assembly and be committed to that local assembly. We need to draw together to renew our strength.

I think that some of the most significant factors in developing any relationship are trust, honor and communication. In our natural friendships, we are careful to consider the other person's feelings. We are attentive to them and spend the necessary time to improve our relationship. If the times we spend together are superficial, then our friendship will remain static or decline.

I remember that early in my marriage my wife and I didn't have any money. I would make hot dogs and pork and beans. We were so poor that we only had one spoon and we'd take turns eating. We were so in love but we were just poor. After a while, we started earning money and began traveling around the world. I started buying her gifts, cars and houses. Then one day I bought her a gift and she began to cry. I asked, "What's wrong with you?" And she replied, "You give me things but you don't give me *you* anymore. I liked it better when we only had one spoon." I said, "baby, don't say that. I will do better. Don't make me go back to one spoon."

You see, in order for our relationships to flourish we must be willing to invest in the other person. The investments we make are in direct correlation to our feelings about that person. We ask ourselves, is this relationship meeting my needs? Our feelings about the person are contingent upon the positive exchanges we have with them. As a result when we experience positive exchanges, we become willing to invest in the relationship. Our relationships are conditional and are based on our level of satisfaction.

You know how it is when you truly love someone. When you genuinely love someone, you have grace for them. The scripture tells us that, "love covers a multitude of sins" (1Pet. 4:8). You can tell when a person actually loves another because they try to cover for them. We meet a young man or woman and as they prove themselves faithful we are willing to go to the next level. They prove themselves at various levels until you say I do. Before this individual came in your life, I'm sure that someone else had tried to get you to say, "I do" but they weren't faithful. And so you said "I don't." I want you to know that the Lord wants to take us to a place, where God has proved Himself in your life.

What would it take for you to say "I do" to God? What would it take for God to prove that He's committed to you? What does it take for you to say "I know without a shadow of a doubt that my God is God?" Now let me tell you, it is fortunate for us that God is not like us. The scripture reminds us that while we were yet sinners Christ died for us. When we are at our worst, God still loves us.

He is able to love us even with His intimate knowledge of all of our shortcomings. Yet that does not mean that God does not have a standard. We know that God offers salvation to the entire world but in order to be saved we are still required to enter into a relationship with him (Rom.10:9). The Lord extends His love as He rains on the just and the unjust. He made provision for every man to inherit the promises of God and then He draws us in by His love (Jer. 31:3).

Although, God moves by His Holy Spirit within our hearts, He still allows us the right to choose and if we reject God's grace, we have to accept the responsibility (consequence) of our choice. Once we have accepted God's grace, like any other relationship, there are ways in which we can deepen our desire for the things of God and enhance the level of intimate fellowship we have with our Savior.

A Deeper Love

You have what you speak. One of the things that you actually need to be critical of is what comes out your mouth because the Bible says life and death are in the power of the tongue. And as you speak negative words to your situation, your situation will deteriorate based on what you say. It will also increase based on what you say. Our faith toward God is one of the most fundamental aspects of our relationship with Him. I realize that it is out of my relationship with God that I speak the word of God. I speak the plan of God. I speak the purpose of God.

The Prophet Elijah spoke that there would be no rain and it did not rain for three and one-half years. Since we discussed faith in a previous section, we will not belabor the point here. However, if we believe God, we will have corresponding actions. We will do what the scripture tells us simply because we believe. Elijah learned to walk by faith. So every day at about five o'clock the Prophet would sit down by the brook and he'd watch the chilly waters run by and then the ravens would appear there and bring the bread first and then bring him a little meat. As the days passed by God proved himself to be reliable and loyal.

God is trying to teach us faith. The enemy is trying to stop us and destroy our faith in God. If the enemy puts a red light in front of you, run it in Jesus name! It's a trick. We're on a journey and it is actually about getting to the place in our walk with God that it matters to us if we are pleasing in His sight. Growing in our love towards God means not crucifying Christ afresh with our actions. It means living a life that reflects God's abiding presence in our hearts. God wants us to honor and esteem Him. We can appreciate God by acknowledging His sovereignty and recognizing that He has power over all things. All things are because God is (Col. 1:16-17).

When we realize that we can do nothing without Him, we will give Him His proper place in our lives. We will be established in every area of life when we revere God (2 Chron. 20:20; 1 Pet. 5:10). When Jesus was teaching the disciples to pray, He said that we must hallow the name of the Lord. To hallow someone is to adore them. We must cultivate a love relationship with our God. He has already instructed us in the methods which lead to having His ear and holding His heart. God tells us to worship and adore Him because He lives in the praise.

King David also understood the power of praise and established the tabernacle of David, where they praised and worshiped the Lord all day. Another communication component of our love relationship with the Lord is praise and prayer. In our prayer time, we should talk with God and be sensitive enough to listen for the answers which He longs to give us (1 Tim. 2:1). When we talk with others, it isn't a one way conversation. Our dialogue with God shouldn't be either. There are also other ways to enhance our relationship with the Lord.

Bible Reading

The word of God is our lifeline. If we don't have the word hidden in our hearts the enemy can attack us and cause us to be defenseless. We cannot depend on having a Bible at hand. We have to come to a place where we are skillful with the weapons that God has given us (2 Tim. 2:15). The scriptures are the truth and as such the cornerstone of our spiritual diet. I have found it an excellent practice to pray before I study my Bible. It seems that as I stir up my spirit in prayer, the Holy Spirit illuminates the scripture as I read. Once the Holy Spirit gives revelation on a scripture, you will never forget it. Our study of scripture will allow us to understand the ways of God. When we know His ways, we will have more of the grace and peace of God operating in our lives (2 Pet. 1:2).

The word of God is a source of comfort and it is also an instrument of war. As our comfort, it is like food as it nourishes us with all the vitamins and minerals we need (the Bread of Life). It reminds us of whose we are and His love for us. The scripture identifies itself as the sword of the spirit and we have to learn to wield our swords skillfully to be effective in combat. You would not trust your life to an army that is not skilled at war. You are a part of that army. We have to realize that the word of God is alive. It is supernatural, not in the sense of spooky or dark; but it is more than, over and above natural (Heb. 4:12). The word of God supersedes our natural sense realm. It has life and it prospers in the place where it is allowed to grow (Isa.55:11; Matt.13). The word of God is the water that washes our minds.

The Lost Art of Meditation

We can help the word to prosper in us as we spend time thinking on the scriptures as we read. We are in such a hurry today that few of us spend any time just sitting before the Lord and thinking about the scriptures. When we are alone we often have some sort of sound distraction: radio, television, computer, or cell phone. I think that we are so uncomfortable with silence that we automatically reach for distractions. That is also the reason why we seldom wait in silence after prayer to hear God's voice.

We also have this idea that meditation is practiced by eastern religions and is not relative to the believer, even though many times in the Psalms the word "Selah" is placed after a verse of scripture and suggests that we think on the subject a while. Meditation does not require that we chant to an idol. It is, however, a silent moment of reflection. What better thing to reflect on than the word of God? When we reflect on the word and mix it with confidence, we will have a crop of spiritual growth. By mercy and truth is iniquity purged (Prov. 16:6).

The Jealous Lover

We touched on this in another chapter of this book but it is advantageous to mention it again. God wants to be first in our lives. Anything that seeks to be equal to or take precedence over God is an idol. For the Lord says that we should have no other gods besides Him. If we set anything before God, it would become an idol. Even our spouses or children can take the place of God if we are not careful. Our ambition, money, education, ministry, gifting, profession, or reputation can become a hindrance to our relationship with the Lord.

We need to allow the true, living God to bring us through, deliver us, mold us, to have fellowship with us (Hab. 2:19). God says there is no breath at all in the midst of it because it is dead. You can fix it up but you can't take it out. It is vain. Idols are false gods. So rather than carrying around a false, dead god; instead of being burdened with the weight of a man-made god, something that we cut out and dressed-up, turn your hearts toward the true and living God. The living God is great! Even His name is mighty and brings deliverance. He is our only solution.

You and I have to understand that the enemy doesn't run our lives. The economy doesn't run our lives. God is our supplier. So, as believers we should not be dismayed at the things which do appear. When we are overtaken by worry about things which we can't control, we can become obsessed and may resort to worldly methods to manage our situations. We don't ever want to be overtaken by our undertakings and be tricked into thinking that every good idea is a God idea. Don't be misled; all of our accomplishments gained outside of Christ will someday perish. We cannot make one step, utter one sound or take one breath without God! He created us and knows us so well that He, more than anyone, knows what is in our best interest (Psalms 139).

What do you do when your stream dries up? Not any old brook but when *your* brook dries up. Regardless of the circumstances, when we are faced with these kinds of trials, we must never lose the two notable truths which are that, God provides water and He can also withhold water. That's what we have to understand. God is the one providing water for the brook to begin with, not our false gods or idols. Contrastingly, He's also the God who can withhold that very same water.

I had a dear friend who was a single parent and she got to the point where she spent more time worrying about her children than anything else. She could hardly pray without being distracted by the fear of what might become of them. She was restless and fearful, needlessly worrying about their past, present and future as if she had control over all the circumstances of their future. Yes, she had input and influence in their lives but God is yet in control of their destiny. The Psalmist reminds us to trust in the Lord, for He is our help and our shield. Many of us are guilty of exalting something above God at one time or another.

Think of it this way. On a very a basic level, we understand that infidelity breaks covenant. Our unfaithfulness to God in the form of idol worship, in the form of our children, our spouses, or our jobs, negatively influences our relationship with Him. The idol in your life can only cause sin to spread into other areas (a little leaven). I think the sin that we continue to carry around affects us because it's like carrying a dead body around. A decaying body holds infection. Just like gangrene, it begins to spread and create a noxious odor. Everyone can smell the poisonous stench except us. We, unfortunately, have become accustomed to the smell. However, there is a remedy. Allow the Holy Spirit and the word of God to wash the infection away and remember that He is only jealous for our protection (2 Cor.11:2).

The Lord continually extends His mercy towards us and draws us by His spirit until we abandon our idols and realize that He is the only living God. If we allow known sin to continue, we will not experience the abundant life that God has given us. We will live in mediocrity and miss many of God's blessings. But, when we place God first, we give Him free reign to accomplish His perfect will; after all, we are the clay, He is the potter. The scripture informs us that God loved us and gave His only son for us. He allows us the privilege of becoming sons also (1 Jn. 3:1). When we deliberately and consciously humble ourselves, we will never forget our source. Is there a relationship in your life right now that God has told you to sever? Then why haven't you? So you have gotten into sin and now you want to find a way to justify it, it won't work. Let it go.

We are Doers of the Word

The things which occupy our thoughts with regularity will eventually become actions if we give power to them. There is a popular quote that says "what consumes your mind controls your life." This is also the reason we need to guard our eyes, ears and mouths. The things we hear, see and say have an effect on our mind and our spirit. The books we read can influence us, as well as the movies we watch and the music we listen to. What may appear harmless can often be deadly. I love music and I listen to all types but sometimes I may have to restrict my intake of certain types of music because of the effect it has on me at that time. We need to know our limitations, because the spirit of God in us, and is too precious for us not to be vigilant.

If we want to learn about money, it is best to inundate our thoughts with every educational tool available on the subject. But what good is it to know about something that is helpful to you and not use the knowledge that you have? The scripture tells us that wisdom is the principle thing because it demonstrates that we have applied the knowledge we have attained.

Remember wisdom is knowledge applied. When we practice the word of God we know others will see the influence of God in us and we will be the living epistles that are read by men. In fact, we are often the only Bible that some may ever read. As we build our relationship through: prayer, reading, speaking, living the word, going to church and keeping God first, we walk in progressive obedience.

Obedience is the Divine Response

To become successful in developing our relationship with the Lord, we must commit. Our ability to obey Him reflects our commitment to the relationship (Luke 6:46-49). Our obedience reaps rewards in the Lord. As we submit to the assignments the Lord gives us, He will trust us with more. He will begin to open doors of opportunity for us to walk through.

There are great doors of opportunity available for the believer to access but as we enter, we have to remember that with those opportunities, come some level of adversity. The good news is that as long as we are doers of the word, we will not be shaken by the adversity. We may bend under pressure but we will never break because the seed of the Holy One lives within us and it is an eternal life generating force. Even though He has given us the victory through Jesus Christ, we may still encounter difficult circumstances in our walk with the Lord.

It is common today for many to believe that a person with strong faith will never encounter adversity. They believe that because they say the right words in the proper order, all things will fall in line. The word tells us to call those things that are not, as though they are so. However, after we have done all that we know to do, when we have fasted, spoken the word of faith and believed it, after we have prayed and praised God and our loved one still goes home to be with the Lord, what do we say then? Are we faithless because we didn't see the manifestation of our desires? Absolutely not! We are stronger than ever and still full of faith because our faith in God is not contingent upon our circumstances. We know that nothing shall separate us from the love of Christ, not our distresses, nor our disappointments can make us believe that God is not who He says that He is (Rom. 8:35-39).

We win in life and in death because we are believers. We only need to examine the lives of the Apostles to affirm that we may live and work for the Lord and yet suffer difficulties. Does our suffering negate the promises of God? Absolutely not! We only need to remember that the battle is already won. We must never forget that God can deliver us but even if He doesn't, He is still God and able to do exceedingly, abundantly above all that we can think or ask according to the power that works within us. We only need to obey Him regardless of the challenges we face.

As we obey God, our love for Him will grow deeper and stronger and He will use us to a greater degree. We gain influence with each step of submission. God wants you to come to a place where you lean on Him like a child in relationship with your parents. How many of us trusted our parents to take care of us and they did what they were supposed to do? Some may have a different story but most of our parents came through for us.

It's like the little girl on a ship. The ship was rocking back and forth and in fact, it looked as if it was going to go under. They woke the little girl up and said, "little girl, little girl, the ship is about to go under." She in turn asked, "Is my daddy on the ship? Well, it's going to be all right because my daddy always comes through for me." When the Lord puts us in a place where we can do nothing but trust Him, He has done us the greatest favor that He could extend to us outside of salvation. The greatest thing that God can do for us is salvation. When we become born again and are filled with the spirit the gifts begin to operate in our life. That's the greatest thing He can do. It is second only to our complete dependence on Him.

In this chapter, we have learned what a deep love relationship with God will require. We can achieve a passionate desire for the things of God if we pursue Him and put Him first. We don't want to use God simply for our benefit. We want to adore Him just because He is God. I think that we have established a solid foundation for our new level of commitment.

Points to Remember:
- *Attendance at a Bible-believing church is important to our development*
- *God wants our trust and honor*
- *He wants us to communicate with Him through prayer*
- *Reading the word of God is another foundation for a strong relationship with Him*
- *Mediation on the Word is a skill we should develop*
- *God desires to be first in our lives*
- *We have to be a doer of the Word and not a hearer only*
- *When we obey God our spiritual walk will be stronger*

Chapter Five
Divine Direction

A friend and I traveled to the downtown area of Detroit to attend a play. We needed to find the theatre. My friend had a navigational system in their car. This was sure to make the trip effortless. Confident that we were following the directions correctly we made every turn exactly as instructed, nevertheless, we arrived at the center of the downtown area but not specifically at the theatre.

There were several distractions downtown like construction, traffic, and pedestrians. As a result my friend became confused. He decided not to follow the navigational directions and tried to find the place from memory. After going in circles for more than ten minutes we pulled over and let the navigator take charge of our trip. We made it to the theatre just in time for the first act. Prior to doing this we found ourselves at a crossroads.

Have you ever been at a crossroad and felt hesitant because you were unsure of which direction to take? You make a turn and wonder if perhaps your destination was straight ahead. You travel a while longer, pensive, looking in every direction for the intended address. Suddenly you realize that you've gone two or three miles in the wrong direction. Becoming frustrated you turn around. Nevertheless, you've wasted valuable time and fuel, which isn't so bad unless you are low on gas or have a time sensitive appointment. If there had been a GPS system in your vehicle, you may have avoided the delay. That is what our lives are like without God's direction. We make false starts and wrong turns. We waste time chasing dreams that are not God's will for our lives. We may even find ourselves pursuing causes that are good but beyond our sphere of influence.

In order to counteract the effects of driving blindly, we need to follow the voice of God's navigational system. We must learn to download the directions the Holy Spirit gives to us. If we listen, God will tell us the turns we need to take for a timely arrival at our destination. The scripture tells us that "there is a way that seems right unto man but the end thereof is death." What we need is divine direction.

What is Divine Direction?

Understanding that direction is guidance, for something to be identified as divine it must originate from a deity. All things that come from God are divine, so divine direction is a course of action or guidance that emanates from God. We discussed the ways that God speaks to His people and how we develop our ability to hear. Once we've heard from God and have received direction, the correct response is obedience. Although man is a free will agent so to speak, we are still in need of direction. Although we have authority to act in God's stead, we still have limited information. Therefore, relying on God's voice or navigational system for direction is a must.

It is only God who knows the end of a thing before the beginning. He is omniscient and desires for man to accomplish His will and fulfill His plan. In order for us to accomplish the purpose of God, we need His guidance. We need to be able to acknowledge His leading and understand His timing. Throughout scripture, God has offered His guidance for two purposes. The first reason is for man to have an abundant life. The second is to bring about His will in the earth. From Genesis to Revelation, God directs man in one form or another. He directed Adam in the garden. He told him what was available to him and what was off limits. However, He never usurped Adam's ability to choose. In life, we will encounter numerous crossroads, it is only by seeking God's wisdom that we are able to select the path to travel.

The Purpose of Divine Direction

Only God knows the plans that He has for each of us. The book of Jeremiah tells us that, "He knows the thoughts that He has for us, thoughts of good and not of evil, to give us an expected end (Jer. 29:11)." In order for us to advance in life, God has endowed each of us with specific gifts and callings. The gifts and callings of God are without regret. Nevertheless, God does have an intended use for them. We are all given our abilities to increase the kingdom of God. Yet, without divine direction, our calling will never operate fully nor will you experience the full manifestation of their power. We need Godly direction to achieve the level of success and satisfaction that God has intended.

God's wants us to be in the right place at the right time. When place, timing, gifting and abilities all coincide, the power of God will be present to advance the kingdom. When we follow the leading of the Lord we are able to be used by Him. We are able to advance His purposes and it increases our level of satisfaction and fulfillment in life. This is what is known as the abundant life. God's gift to us is the ability to share them with others for the purpose of abundant life.

The Leading of the Lord

We learn to follow the leading of the Lord through our experiences with Him. We must condition ourselves to place our spiritual ears close to God's mouth. That way, we can receive His instructions. This process is much like children learning to walk. It requires practice. Receiving direction from God means becoming familiar with His voice, in other words, we may think we are being directed to do something and find that our efforts are fruitless.

If we have no results, even after the proper application of time and effort, then the endeavor was probably not prompted by the leading of the Lord. God wants us to flourish and be fruitful. That's why He wants us to stay connected to the vine or the voice. As we are connected to Him and He prunes or challenges us, so we are more productive. God's direction is always attached to His purpose. God will not scatter His efforts, He is concise. It is God's will to bring heaven to earth. God is organized, focused and wants us to be also.

A dear friend of mine was on vacation at Niagara Falls. She'd been praying for answers about her business. Her desire was to accomplish more than she had in the past. As any good business person would, she made a list of goals. No matter what she did, she just couldn't seem to make much of them happen. While standing, on the Canadian side of Niagara Falls, watching the water tumble down in great waves, she noticed the power of the water. Niagara is a natural fall and yet through the ingenuity of man, natural power had been harnessed for electricity. In that instant, God spoke to her. She knew how and on what she should center her business efforts on. In the same way, the water was harnessed at the Falls; she would be like a laser and penetrate through the obstacles that had stood in her path.

Divine direction is focused energy pointed toward specific targets. God does not cause confusion. His presence, voice and direction bring light, clarity, precision and definition. Satan, will try to cause pressure from outside sources to muddle our perception to make us miss the leading of the Lord.

How do I Know When it is God?

In the previous chapter, we talked about hearing the voice of God. We discovered the many ways God leads His people. In the Bible, people used all sorts of methods to hear a direction from God. For example in the Old Testament some men consulted prophets, drew straws and even tried to swindle God in an effort to find His will. There are examples of drawing straws or casting in the book of Acts. The people were with one accord and waiting for the promise of the Holy Spirit. The disciples cast lots for Judas' replacement. The scripture records that the lot fell to Matthias and he was numbered with the eleven apostles. Once the Holy Spirit arrived, the people were energized and received power from on high. As New Testament believers, we are blessed with the Holy Spirit who leads us into all truth. The Holy Spirit is our guide and our teacher. He shows us things to come. We can be confident that He is leading us the right way.

How Can We be Sure?

It's not always easy, just like my friend who drove us to that downtown area mentioned above. We may be overwhelmed by outside pressure. When enough is applied, we may succumb to it and be taken off course. This is because each one of us has what's called a familiar spirit that follows us around. This is a demonic spirit from hell. Familiar spirits gather information about you like a private investigator. The devil is not omnipresent like God;

nonetheless he has a dossier on you. He uses this information to attack in the areas of your weakness. Most people don't move more than seven to ten miles from the place they were born. This allows the enemy to have enough intelligence on them to hold them down. That's why people can often have more success sometimes by relocating. Demons there don't know you nor do they have any information on your propensities.

The only way to avoid the trap of outside pressure is to have constant communion with the Holy Spirit. That communion can only be found in a consistent prayer life. Jesus is our primary example of what our prayer life should look like. He sought time alone with the Father every day. He replenished His power in prayer and communion with His father. Just like Jesus, we have to pray constantly. When we endeavor to develop our prayer lives, the power of the Holy Spirit will increase in us like it did Jesus and His disciples. With an awesome prayer life we will be able to do great things for the kingdom. As the scripture tells us, the works that Jesus did, we will do also and much greater. As a byproduct of our prayer life, we will be accustomed to the leading of the Lord in our lives.

The Ways He Leads

God often leads us through confirmation or what the Bible calls a "witness". There is always authentication of God's leading. We received this in a variety of ways; one is through other people's verbal confirmation. It is "out of the mouth of two or three witnesses that every word is established (2 Cor. 13:1)." Confirmation may come in the form of scriptures, dreams and prophetic words. Plus we can never discount the importance of relationships. Ultimately, God wants to get us to a place where we lean on Him. God orchestrates circumstances to get our attention and move us in the direction that He wants us to go.

I have a dear friend who was called to the ministry. He knew that he was gifted to be a pastor but he wanted to do things in his own way and in his own timing. His desire was to shepherd a certain type of people and to deliver his message in a particular way. He concluded that once everything was in perfect order he would launch the ministry. In his mind, all things would flow, and the mega church would shortly come to pass. Eventually, my pastor friend did become the pastor of a great church but first he had to go through the fire.

He lost his job and his beautiful new home. His family also experienced satanic attack. After going through all of that he abandoned his own ideas of how things should be and simply walked in the will of God. Am I saying that God brought those things on him? Absolutely not, however, God did allow those events to help shape him into the man he was designed to be. I Peter 5:10 reminds us that after we have suffered a while, God will make us perfect. He will establish us, strengthen us and settle us, just like he did for my pastor friend.

The Importance of Relationship

God also uses the wise counsel from family, friends and our spiritual leadership to speak to us. There is nothing wrong with asking for help. God uses others to fulfill His will in the earth. On the flip side we've all heard stories about foolish friends leading another astray. The company we keep defines us. I focus on friendship. We can't select our family members, we can only accept them. Conversely, we chose our friends. Close relationships, no matter how hard we try, will have an effect on our thoughts. Thoughts influence actions and destinies can be hindered by wrong relationship. That is why our friendships matter. They help us discover the will of God. Prov. 27:17 says that "iron sharpens iron, so a man sharpens the continence of his friend". Our friends should help us arrive at the place that God has ordained for us.

God also gives us great spiritual leaders. The Bible reminds us to comply with our leaders so that their leadership doesn't become grieved. If leaders are grieved because of us, we are not profitable by it. Just as friendships have an influence on us, our spiritual leaders have an influence on us. If we can't submit to leadership we will not have the results that God desires. We will always fall short of our potential. We may have many gifts and talents but they will remain idle because leader, spiritual or otherwise, does not want a rebel in their organization trying to take over.

What does our relationship to leadership have to do with our destiny? There are many powerful examples of the benefit of good leadership in scripture. One is the story of David at the Cave of Adullam. David fled from Saul, who was trying to find and kill him. He took refuge in a cave. People heard about where David was and joined him. The word tells us that everyone who was distressed, in debt and discontented gathered themselves to David, who was destined to be king of Israel but wasn't yet.

While under David's leadership the men who had once been referred to as discontented became mighty men of valor. They were no longer in the distressed condition. The result of submitting to good leadership is that we will reach our potential. Good leadership is another means of receiving direction from God.

God, I Missed It. What Do I Do Now?

Don't panic all is not lost. The same God who started a good work in you will see it completed. (Phil. 1:6). He also promised to perfect the things that concern us. If we find that we've missed God's leading, we simply need to make the necessary corrections. Then get back on track. You get back on track by repenting for the mistakes you made and ask God to forgive you. Once you have done that, you are on your way to Destiny! However, the enemy will try to condemn you for mistakes. Satan's voice may say, "You should have known better." Perhaps you should have, but condemnation is just another trick. You are wasting valuable time that could be spent building the kingdom.

I am not suggesting that there are no consequences for mistakes or sin. However, God still loves you and will restore you the time you wasted. He will replenish what was stolen. We serve a God who's already alive in our tomorrow. We are limited by time, however, God is not. He stepped out of time. That's why they call Him the Alpha and the Omega, the beginning and the end. He knows how a situation will end before it begins. He knew it before the foundation of the world.

He was aware that Adam and Eve were going to commit sin in the garden before the world was formed. That's why the Bible says that the Lamb was slain before the foundation of the world. He knew you were going to mess up. That is the whole understanding of forgiveness. God knows that you and I are flesh, so He prepared a Lamb to cleanse us and wash us. Just like little children, no matter how clean you get them, you know they are going to mess up. That's why good parents keep extra clothes for them.

Before the dawn ever breaks, the Lord already knows what's going on and He has placed what we need in our path. That's why we should ask God for direction. Regardless of the circumstances, God has already prepared the route I should take.

On the Right Path

He knows where you are and what provisions you need. However, He requires us to ask anyway. He wants you to know that He answers you and He cares for you as an individual. He will direct you to the place where your need can be met. That's why our morning prayer time is important. It is the time when God gives us direction. In my opinion, the perfect time for prayer is the morning. He guides our day and our steps. The Bible says, the "footsteps of the righteous are ordered of the Lord." God longs to tell you where to go but you have to ask Him for directions.

God directed Elijah and he did what God told him to do. In other words, when God called Elijah, he simply stepped out on faith and obeyed God. When you and I hear God, it's not the time to reason or use theological debate. It's time to hear and obey.

"I want to be more pliable Lord", that should become our anthem. When God closes doors or changes our relationships will we follow His leading? If we trust Him, we will follow Him. Trust is built over time and through experience. We only need to remember that the One who is leading us knows the outcome. Not only does He know the conclusion but has plans to give us the best possible end.

God knows the thoughts that He has toward us and He wants us to have an excellent end. I want the ending that God has for me. I want to walk in the sphere of influence that he has given me. When we earnestly desire to do God's will, we do so with an attitude of compliance. We should not be rebellious.

Divine direction gives us what the scripture calls the immutability of His counsel. Counsel is guidance or a deliberate resolution. Immutability is something that doesn't change. We can depend on God, He does not change. We can trust that He is bringing us to an excellent end. We know this because God is certain. He knows where we are going. He causes all things to work together for our good. All that's left for us to do is travel the path He has set for us by combining the word of God with faith; we can actively pursue our destinies.

Following His Lead

In this chapter, we have learned that God has a navigational system for our lives. If we use the system, we can save time, money and heartache. As freewill agents, we chose to live dependent or independent of God. If we want to avoid walking blindly, we should allow the Lord to direct our steps. In the next segment, we will look at ways we can:

- Actively participate
- Grow spiritually
- Learn to become a spirit-led person
- Develop our relationship with the Lord

Points to Remember:

- The Holy Spirit is our guide and teacher
- Divine direction comes from God
- Divine direction advances the kingdom and provides the believer with a more abundant life
- Outside pressure is a trap
- Divine direction focuses our efforts
- A consistent prayer life develops our sensitivity to God
- God confirms His word
- Relationships influence us
- Aligning with Godly leadership benefits us

Chapter Six
Positioned to Receive Instructions, Having an Ear to Hear

Does God Speak to Everyone

Some people believe God only speaks to Christians. I remember hearing God as a young man before I was saved and established a relationship with God. I was a senior in high school and walking with a group of friends, we were coming from the fair grounds and we had knives on us. Suddenly, I got the distinct impression that we should dispose of our knives, so we did. Shortly after we disposed of the knives the police stopped us. We were all searched and placed in back of the squad car. If the police had found knives on us, we would have been arrested. If we hadn't followed the impression or been fearful about what I heard I can only imagine what might have happened to us.

When God gives us an impression about something, a couple of things may happen: we may feel assurance that the path we're on is the right one or we have a sense of danger regarding the way. There are numerous accounts of people who felt a sense of foreboding about going in a certain direction. However, by paying attention to the voice they heard, some were able to avoid danger. Others who listened or followed the impression they received discovered their destiny. Often impressions come with an uneasy feeling regarding a particular course of action. We may find that our peace about a situation is gone and we're unsure about a decision.

I remember a few years ago, a woman who was considering marriage to the man she was dating. However, she wanted to marry a Christian, so she prayed and sought the Lord. Although she sensed that the relationship was not God's best for her, she was experiencing financial difficulties and the man she was dating offered to help her. She allowed the stress of her circumstances to cause her to enter into a bad decision. She went ahead and married the man, even though she believed he was not her husband. She found out the hard way that God is always right. Why would God allow her to enter into that marriage? God did not violate her free will. Instead, she dismissed the revelation that she received from God. When we trust God, we position ourselves to receive his best.

Another Revelation

God leads us through difficulties so we can learn to submit to His will and lean on Him. We cannot be supported by our own understanding. As such there are times when He'll put us in a situation that our mind can't figure it out.

There's a story in the Bible about a Godly man from Judah who was a powerful prophet. Once, the king of the land was angry with the man and tried to grab him violently with his hands. Due to the power that the prophet had the king's hand shriveled up and remained deformed until the prophet prayed for him. Afterwards the king's hand was restored. This prophet walked in the power of God because he heard from the Lord.

One time this same prophet received very specific instructions from God to go into a certain city but not to eat or drink anything or go into anyone's house while he was in the city. At first he was obedient, but then an older prophet came along and convinced him that he too had heard from the Lord. The old prophet told the younger that God essentially changed his mind, meaning that it was now okay for the younger prophet to stop, eat and rest. The story goes on to say that the old prophet was lying to the younger. As a result of the young man's disobedience, he died on his return trip home, after realizing the mistake he made.

What we learn from this story is that we must be able to hear God for ourselves. It also reaffirms the Bible is the final authority in the life of the believer. The word of God contains the mind of God. In our quest to develop a hearing ear towards God, there are things we should consider. We have to think about the things that distract us from hearing God's voice and cause disobedience.

How Do We Hear from God?

Hearing from God may be different for each of us. He speaks to us in many ways. First of all, He speaks through

His word or the Bible. The word of God is truth. It's a measuring tool for any voice we think we hear. If the voice or direction we've heard doesn't coincide with the word, then it is not God. What about issues that are not found in scripture? Like where we should live, work, or who we should marry. How do we hear God's direction on these important life concerns?

One way that God speaks to us about these matters is through an audible voice. You may think that hearing the audible voice of God is impossible. However, God can do anything He wants. In fact, there's an example in the Bible of when God used a donkey to speak to a prophet. Another example is the prophet Samuel who heard God's audible voice. Even in the New Testament, God spoke to Apostle Paul in an audible voice. I am not suggesting this is the typical style of hearing the voice of God, I'm simply saying it's possible.

I was at a business meeting once. The table where I was seated was full. Everyone was quiet except for one person. As that person was speaking I heard the word liar being whispered into my left ear. It was so clear that I turned to look at the person on my left side; however, that person was not speaking to me. How was this possible? Who spoke to me? In that moment, I knew I'd just heard the voice of God. That information gave me valuable insight about the person. Knowing this kept me from entering into a very poor business decision that day.

The Ways Which God Speaks

The first and most important way that God speaks to His people is through His word. *Logos* is the Greek word for the written word of God. The word of God is the final authority. We should mediate on the word of God, expecting revelation. Along with the logos word of God, there is the rhema word of God. *Rhema* is a Greek word which denotes a God breathed personal word from the Lord. The rhema word may come to us through dreams, visions, prophecy, revelation in nature, or He simply speaks through the words and actions of others. When we are overwhelmed by the activities of everyday life, God will have to get our attention some other way.

Dreams

God sometimes speaks to us in vivid and memorable dreams. Dreams can offer direction. Or tell us how and when God wants to fulfill His plan. In the Old Testament, Joseph, the son Jacob, had a dream that revealed his destiny. His only mistake was sharing it with his brothers. In the New Testament, Mary's husband Joseph had a dream which alerted him to the danger ahead. He changed course and preserved the life of Jesus our savior.

Visions

God may also allow us to have visions. The difference between a dream and a vision is that we are awake when we experience a vision and asleep when we have a dream. I had a vision once while on vacation. I was in my room praying, when suddenly I saw people being marched to hell. There were several people lined shoulder to shoulder with oxbows around their necks. They walked together and were driven by demons. Yet the most troubling notion about the vision was that none of them seemed to notice that they were captive. They walked along as if they didn't have a care. The ground all around them was dusty and as they continued to walk lines and lines of them tumbled over a cliff. I asked the Lord what it meant. He said that those were the people of the world. They were oblivious to their predicament without Jesus. The vision led me back to the Bible. I began to hear the voice of God speak. Some people hear more clearly as God speaks to their hearts and communicates His will and desires.

The Prophetic

The prophetic word can transform lives. When I talk about the prophetic, I am talking about the way God communicates with His people. I can recall several instances when the Lord spoke and it came to pass. A young pregnant woman in our congregation was told by her doctors that her child would be deformed. She was distraught. The word of the Lord came through my wife and my wife prophesied that the woman would have a normal child and it came to pass. On another occasion, I prophesied to two other young women whose doctors told them they would not be able to conceive. After the word of God was prophesied, both women were able to conceive. The word of God came to pass!

When I first received the Lord into my life, I didn't have anyone to train me in the prophetic. My entire relationship with God was trial and error. I just said, okay I'm going to try this, and I would try it. For example, I was crossing the street one day on my way home when a woman walked by, as she walked by, the wind blew her dress up, not all the way but the air blew under it. Afterward, the wind subsided and the dress came back down. However, to me it didn't look like her dress anymore, her dress appeared in the form of a baby. The Lord spoke to me and said that she is pregnant. The Lord said to tell her that she's pregnant. I told her and she started crying. Later she brought her husband to our home and asked me tell him what I'd said to her. So I replied, "You are going to have a baby." Interestingly enough the couple had been praying for a child. Several months later the child was born, just like the Lord said.

During the early years of flowing in the prophetic, God often spoke to me about random people walking past me. I'd walk up to them and prophecy. Any number of things would happen, sometimes people cried, and some took off running. There were even times I'd take off running because the stupid things I'd said. Incidences like that happened all the time. The Lord would tell me to go to the mall, so I'd go and just sit there and watch people. We can look all around us and see God's handiwork in the earth.

God Speaks Through Nature

One can sit on the shores of the ocean and see the works of the almighty God. It is evident in the sand beneath our feet and the vastness of the sea before us. How can someone look at the Northern lights as they illuminate the night sky and not meditate on God's creation and His matchless power? The scripture tells us that the heavens declare the glory of God; and the firmament shows His handiwork. The vastness and wonder of the universe speaks to the eternal nature of our God. It is during these times of reflection that we can often best hear from God. As we acknowledge His glory and are awed by His majesty. His responds to us for acknowledging his splendor is that we get to feel His presence.

God knows the final outcome of everything even before it happens. He wants the same for His people, for us to know what He knows, not for us to walk around guessing what's next. His wish is that we know His will concerning our lives. We should not be in the dark when we have the Holy Spirit inside of us screaming to be heard. I Cor. 2:9, says that "eyes have not seen, nor ears heard, neither has it entered into the heart of man, what God has prepared for them that love Him", but God has revealed it unto us by His spirit He wants us to hear His voice. He wants us to have knowledge of His will. If that's true what prevents us from hearing the voice of God?

Why Can't I Hear Him?

We can become so preoccupied that God has to find alternate means to communicate with us. We have established that there are several ways we can hear from God. There are people who believe that they don't hear from God. We are often distracted by the cares of this world. The enemy is deliberate and relentless in his attempts to take our focus off of the things of God. He chokes out the word of God with the lust of the flesh, the lust of the eyes and the pride of life.

Time spent alone in the presence of God is what brings His Glory. God is looking for someone who wants to be with Him and share times of intimacy and fellowship just as we have with people. God gave us many gifts because He is good.

God allows man the grace to hear from Him. However it takes practice like anything else that takes practice, the ability to hear God can be developed. We can liken this concept to muscle conditioning, it takes discipline. Hearing God is a discipline. If we are not experienced in hearing God's voice, we may not hear Him clearly.

Positioning Ourselves to Hear

When we spend time reading the word, it's good to form a habit of taking a "Selah" or taking time to think about what we have just read. If we can take the time to allow the Holy Spirit to give us revelation on the scriptures, the word will become relevant to our life. We will also need to limit distractions. You may find yourself reading your word and falling asleep. You weren't sleepy before you started reading but suddenly you just can't keep your eyes open. It might be helpful to identify your most energetic time of the day and spend that time in prayer and meditation.

Someone asked me, if we need a physical position to hear God. We don't have to kneel, or lay down to hear from God. We can be walking in the mall or driving in our cars and still hear the Lord. When our spirit is conditioned to the sound of His voice we can hear Him anywhere. Much of the conditioning that is necessary to hear God's voice will happen during prayer. A well-developed prayer life will make us familiar with God's presence. We will learn when to speak and when to listen. As we pay attention to God during our specific prayer time, we will become accustomed to hearing his voice at other times. Our ability to hear God is also strengthened as we pray in our prayer language or pray in tongues.

The Apostle Paul said that praying in an unknown tongue edifies the believer. To edify is to instruct, enlighten, encourage or to improve. By praying in tongues, we speak directly to God. He imparts encouragement and strength. Our ability to hear is increased.

Do We All Hear His Voice the Same Way?

No. We don't all hear the voice of God the same way. God knows each of us intimately. He knows our personalities because He made us. As the manufacturer knows His product; God knows His creation. Because He knows us, He is able to speak to us in ways only we understand. God is awesome. He can create a snowflake that is completely unlike any other. He creates man with fingerprints and characteristics that are unique. God speaks to our hearts.

For example, in the book of I Samuel we learn about Samuel as a young boy in the temple. He lived with a blind priest and his two good-for-nothing sons. Samuel was not familiar with God but this did not prevent him from hearing. What about the great men and women of God in the bible, who started movements and waged wars to obey the voice of God? For example, Elijah the prophet heard the voice of God and received instruction that helped him get the provision he required to sustain him. The Bible says that the word of the Lord came to Elijah to go to the brook Cherith and he would be fed by ravens. It does not say how God spoke to Him but we know that he recognized the voice of the Lord.

Recognition and Responsibility

Once we become familiar with God's voice we are required to respond appropriately. Throughout the scriptures, there are stories about people who heard from God and responded; some correctly and others incorrectly. The proper response to God is obedience. If we are unsure about this notice we need only consider the story of King

Saul. The results of his disobedience were devastating. Saul lost the kingdom because he chose not to obey. His final act of disobedience came after the Prophet Samuel gave him explicit orders to destroy the Amalekites, Agag, their king and all of their possessions.

As we recall, Saul decided to keep the best stuff for the people and he would keep King Agag alive. Saul thought it would be better if he made a sacrifice from the plunders of war to the Lord. After this last decision to disobey, God sent in the Prophet Samuel who loved and supported Saul. Nevertheless, God instructed Samuel to confront King Saul for his defiance. Samuel obeyed God. However, Saul never did obey. As a result Saul was unable to hear God's voice again. After this King Saul consulted psychics for guidance. Eventually this practice led to Saul's death and the detriment of all his descendants except one. He was replaced by David as king. There will always be consequences for disobeying what we know to be His will.

The Proper Response

The proper response to hearing the voice of God is to obey. The Bible says obedience is better than sacrifice. If we compare King Saul to King David it is clear that David was obedient. He was not a perfect man by any means, but his willingness to recognize his wrong and correct it gave him an advantage with the Lord. King David was quick to repent and confronted evil, even his own. We are probably all familiar with David's betrayal of Uriah the Hittite. It was a devastating sin, with far reaching consequences. However, David could hear from the Lord. He also listened to wisdom like that of Prophet Nathan. David accepted God's judgment, turned from the sin he committed and he never did it again. Many times in David's life, he observed the ways of God and changed his behavior.

The Final Test

God needs someone to cover the city tonight in prayer and it's your turn. When He wakes you up stand there and intercede, stand on the wall. Don't go to sleep. Don't try to find someone to take your place, be steadfast in your assignment and it will amplify your hearing. God expects us to have the divine response of obedience when we hear His voice. The small steps we take to obey will develop our relationship with Him. As we practice obeying the voice of God, our relationship with Him will deepen. As we have examined in the previous chapter, when hearing from God, He will lead us by His divine direction. Direction is what we need in order to keep our lives in alignment. We won't waste time doing things that God hasn't called us to when we follow his direction.

Points to Remember:

- **The ability to hear the voice of God will allow us to increase in the knowledge of God and give us understanding for our life**

- God has given every man the ability to hear from Him in one form or another
- There are various ways which we can hear from God
- He speaks to believers and non-believers alike
- We have to remove the hindrances that will keep us from hearing from God
- Hearing from God is a spiritual muscle
- Whatever we practice will become stronger and more defined

Chapter Seven
There is an Expected End for You Purpose and Destiny

Three women were walking along a dusty road, in the hot sun, carrying the sorrows of life along with all the belongings they owned in the sacks on their shoulders. Their faces were drawn from hunger and the creases of their eyes were filled with dust. They came to a fork in the road and it was there that the oldest of the three bid the two younger ones goodbye. The women hugged, held each other close and cried. The older woman gave the younger ones her consent. She said, "It is time for you to return to your families." Both of the younger women insisted that they would stay with their elder and begged her not to send them back. The older woman pulled her shawl tightly around her head and once again, told the young women to walk away from her and move on to their future.

They came together in a circle with their arms wrapped around each other and wept bitterly; the pain of their voices traveling through the air. Each of them thought of the difficulties they faced during the past few years. They moved from one place to another. There never seemed to be enough to go around. Even when their husbands were working they still had a hard time making ends meet. Eventually, their husbands toiled and wore themselves down until one by one they died.

One of the younger women kissed the older woman and told her goodbye. The other young woman stood by the old woman's side and she pleaded with her not to send her away. "Please," she said, "I will never leave you. Wherever you go, I will go. Your people will be my people and your God will be my God; only death will separate us (Ruth 1:16)." That was a powerful statement of faith coming from a woman who was in a barren country and had no real direction. Yet she still trusted in the old woman who she had lived and suffered with until now. The women continued on their journey until they reached their destination in Bethlehem. The story of Ruth is a narrative in the fulfillment of purpose and destiny. The young woman Ruth became the mother of one of the descendants of our Lord. She realized her purpose and fulfilled her destiny.

Destiny and Purpose Working Together

When I searched for an understanding of the word purpose, I found the simplest and most concise definitions were the aim and design. The design suggests the original intent for a specific thing. Destiny is the ultimate fulfillment of the design. I could not ignore the story of Ruth, a Moabite, when having a discussion about purpose and destiny. Ruth 2:16 says, "And, let fall also some of the handfuls of purpose for her and leave them, that she may glean them and rebuke her not." This scripture reference to purpose was talking about wheat. However wheat was the provision that was left for Ruth but it was because she was in the place of purpose that she found it. Before He formed us in our mother's womb, God knew us and had wonderful plans (purpose) and destiny for us (Jerimiah 1:5). Although Ruth was not a Hebrew, God chose her to be part of the lineage of Jesus; she fulfilled her destiny.

We see that Ruth experienced hard times. She lost her husband, her home and was no longer with her biological family and did not have a child of her own to eventually help take care of her. Even when she chose to stay with her mother-in-law, she worked to care for the both of them, and went to find wheat for them in order to have food each week.

Like Ruth, all of us have had difficult times in our lives, some more than others. Some seem to move from one trauma to another. However, what we can learn from Ruth is to find our God-given purpose so there is strength and provision during the tough times. She went from famine to reaping. To reap is to obtain as a result of your own efforts. She progressed from reaping to gleaning. Gleaning means to pick-up bit by bit. Ruth went from gleaning to abundance. We can all expect to glean the rewards and live a life of abundant grace as we move to destiny.

One might ask the question, what should our aim be and for what intentions were we designed? Unfortunately unless it is by divine revelation, I can't tell you and neither can anyone else. I have some excellent news: The one who made you, the master designer, your creator, knows what He designed you for! There is a scripture that says the whole duty of man is to praise God, and one might initially think that is referencing singing; dancing or lifting hands to worship, and that is part of it. Actually, that starts the pathways to learning the individual purpose as you give your heart to God in praise and worship for who he is. We also learn purpose by living a lifestyle of praise which is thankfulness and learning about God. Our willingness to conform to the purpose of God, by what we see and learn from his word for us, will determine the length of time it will take us to accomplish our destiny. It took the Israelites forty years to get in divine alignment. When purpose and destiny meet it will produce the power of God.

Corporate Purpose

As a body of believers, the church has a corporate purpose and destiny in God. When we speak of the church, also known as the body of Christ, we are not talking about the building. It's the believers who form the church, the "ecclesia," or the "called out ones." The primary focus of the church is to manifest the kingdom of God. We pray for the kingdom of God to come on earth because we want the purpose and will of God to be fulfilled in the earth. When we grow in knowledge of Christ, we also pray for grace and peace. The Bible also says the body is held together by that which "every member" supplies. Meaning, we have a collective purpose as well as an individual purpose. As believers, the love of God is how we are known. For example, Jesus said that men will know we are his disciples because of the love we share with one another. We are nothing without the love of God operating in us. As a matter of fact, the Apostle Paul says that our works, our efforts or any of the things we say or do is just a bunch of noise if we are not operating from a place of love (I Cor. 13:1). Love is a signature mark of our corporate destiny.

God has a brilliant plan for the church to fulfill corporate destiny. Ephesians 4:7-13 says he gave "gifts to men". These gifts are in the form of apostles, prophets, evangelists, pastors and teachers. This references the governmental offices of the church and commonly referred to as the five-fold ministry. This is important, because it references how the body of Christ is supposed to grow, become equipped and eventually function under the direction of the head of all things, which is under Christ. It is from these "gifts" that we learn to renew our minds and buffet our bodies (Rom. 12:2; 2 Cor. 10:5). We also learn how to possess our vessels in sanctification and honor (1 Thes. 4:4) and to eventually want to walk worthy of the Lord and produce the fruit of the spirit (Col. 1:10).

There is another signature mark for the church moving to corporate purpose and that is the prayer of becoming "one" as seen in Jesus' prayer prior to being crucified. Simply put, as the natural body cannot move and function without working together, the church will not make destiny without the collective purposes.

The corporate destiny of the church also requires maturity, however, this comes over time and as individual members are in place within the local body of Christ and growing together in love (Eph. 4:16). The fruit of the Spirit grows in our lives we mature and takes responsibility to cultivate the fruit. Although God gives gifts of the Spirit, that does not substitute living a personal walk/journey to know God, conform to His will and to walk in obedience. When we desire to have a greater production of fruit we will have to develop it through our faith and the operation of faith is by love. As we walk in the spirit and produce its fruit, we will destroy the works of the flesh and magnify the kingdom of God (Matt. 22:37-40). When we demonstrate the love of God to a dying world we are lifting Jesus up and He draws men to Himself. The world does not care how much we know but they do want to know how much we care. Ultimately, the individual and corporate destinies will both work together to "destroy the works of the devil" as Jesus stated in (John 3:8).

Fight

As we lay hold to the purpose of God for our lives, and in becoming a part of the body of Christ, we will be sustained through adversity, disappointment and sorrow. We honor the Lord by conforming to His plan for us and maintaining that His word and plans for our lives are true and worth fighting about. We must refuse to mimic and rehearse what the enemy says; the enemy is a liar and an accuser. He comes as a thief to kill, steal and destroy (John 10:10). It's pathetic to be defeated by him because Jesus has already won the victory and called us overcomers (I John 5:4). God has provided many love letters (as it were) via his word and states over and over his love and wonderful intentions over us. Jesus displayed this lavishly in healing, delivering, opening blinded eyes and empowering people. He openly stated that "he that hath seen me has seen the Father" (John 14:9). It's important to know that rehearsing God's words is the way to enforce and walk in the purpose and ultimate destiny for our lives.

We Need Each Other

One of the ways to see the body of Christ and our need for one another is in this simply story. There was an old man who lay dying in his bed. The sheets and blanket were wet from sweat. He groaned and tossed from side to side in pain. His wife stood on one side of the bed looking helpless. His pastor was on the other side of the bed praying feverishly. The pastor told the old man about another preacher he knew who had the gift of healing in his hands. The pastor told the old man to hold on while he ran to get the preacher with the healing hands. The pastor ran to the preacher who was in the fields working. The pastor told him the story and asked him to come quick the old man was dying. The preacher dropped what he was doing and ran to help the old man. The preacher had seen God use him many times before to heal the sick. He wanted to share his gift with all who were in need.

They arrived at the old man's house and went upstairs to the bedroom. The pastor introduced the old man to the preacher and he told him that the preacher would lay his hands on him and he would be fine. Well, that old man took one look at that preacher's dirty hands and he shook his head "no" and mustered a few words as he told the pastor, "I don't want him to touch me; his hands are dirty." Needless to say, the old man died that day. We should learn to recognize the purpose of others in our lives and passionately pursue our destiny.

Understanding Who You are in the Lord

As believers our purpose is in Christ. In order to find your true purpose, we must first have a relationship with Jesus; not just a relationship based on knowledge of Christ as Savior but a relationship where we begin to mature and grow in sensitivity to the Spirit of God. As we are sensitive to the leading of the Spirit, we will begin to discern our areas of gifting naturally and spiritually. We will be able to see the things that we love and actually do well. Our gift will make room for us. As new believers, we may be unable to digest much of the meat of the word because it is too powerful for us at that time. As we grow we become able to digest more of the word and begin to get wisdom and understanding about ourselves and our purpose in God.

Many have asked what is my purpose or what am I here for? In order to understand our purpose in God, we have to spend time in His presence and become sensitive to the leading of the Holy Spirit. We can slow the process of our development if we are not being led by the spirit. In other words, we can't be hardheaded or disobedient to God if we want to grow and advance.

When our growth is stunted, we become more concerned with other people's affairs more than God. We desire our brothers' or sisters' gift instead of asking God to help us to develop our own gifts. We desire the blessing of God more than we desire God. We become more concerned with the positions of men than with the office of God. When we rebel it also promotes slow growth within us. If you have been rebellious and you know it, repent. Our willingness to confess our wrongs will increase our growth cycle in God. So, be led of the Spirit and allow the small, still voice of the spirit of God to lead you to the gleaning fields of your purpose. Jesus said "my sheep know my voice" so it is natural for the born-again believer to hear and move under God's direction (John 10:27).

Don't allow anyone to rebuke you for having a hunger and thirst for your purpose. If those who have attached themselves to you don't want to glean the purpose of God for their life, pray for them to be delivered from the affliction of stunted growth, but put some distance in between you and them. What if Ruth had gone the way of Orpah? We would have probably never heard of her again. Our purpose was set from the foundation of the world (Jer.

1:5). If we look at the analogy of a manufacturer we realize they know best how to operate its product. He knows how it was put together and how much pressure it can take before reaching the breaking point. How much more can we expect the one who created us to know what is best for us? Let's follow His instructions.

Fulfilling Destiny

Let's look at Elijah again. He is about to find out that God has another place already prepared for him. God had instructed the widow to sustain him (I King 17:9).

We can be confident that God has a destiny for all of us. Our destiny or the ultimate fulfillment of our purpose becomes clearer as we progress in our walk with the Lord. God says that there are some things He has for you that you don't even have to work for and you can't buy it because it is not for sale. It will be by His grace. Not because you were so good or because you deserved it. It will be a testament in your life of His graciousness and desire for you to have it; just because He is good!

When the brook dries up, it could mean that God has a new way that He wants to bless you or that He has another place for you. God can use or allow events in our lives to get our attention when we walk outside His Will; however, there are times when He lets the brook dry up in the midst of your serving Him, meaning it's not that you have done something wrong. Elijah obeyed God's will and was walking in God's Plan but the brook still dried up.

So if the brook dries up we can realize that God is pleased with us and desires to take us to a new and better thing; it's an invitation to get into His presence. It's an invitation to bless Him and praise Him and get closer to Him to hear His voice and take His direction. There isn't a need to question your faithfulness or God's intentions; it's just time for a new season and higher level. It is okay for God show you that He has something new for you.

God knows us and He knows that we are reluctant to leave a place where everything is going perfect. When things are going well, we might not want to let go of our current situation. However God wants better. Too many times we become satisfied with good. Therefore He dries up our brook causing us to be willing to go where He leads. He'll get our attention. Sometimes God allows the brook to dry up because we're guilty of trusting our brook more than we trust Him. The lesson here; don't let a favorable situation become the enemy of the great things that God has for you.

The scripture says there's a good, perfect and an acceptable will of God (Romans 12:2). What happens is that we get into one spot and we don't get any better. We don't get the perfect will of God because we're sanctified and satisfied. God has a better plan for your life. He is shaking things up in order for you to get into His perfect will.

On the road of purpose and destiny, we still have to become. This means we will go through things to make us grow-up, increase our faith and build character. There are also things that the Lord will have to separate us from to assist us in reaching our destiny. For example, Jesus was "led" into the wilderness by the Spirit (Luke 4:1). He spent time fasting, praying and was also tempted by the devil during that time (Luke 4:13). We also have to be conformed to the image of His dear son. There are many names for the place of our making: the refiner's fire, the potter's wheel and the threshing floor. It is the place of separation where God separates you from your habits. He will separate you from some of your friends, from your lover and from yourself. Yes, even from your desires, until your desires become His. It is the place where He gets the dross off. It is where the alabaster box is broken and our props are removed. It is the place where purpose becomes personal.

If you embrace this process, you won't leave His presence empty. You will be filled with His anointing for your purpose. If you give yourself to Him in this season (sow to the spirit) you will reap. He will equip you for His service. Don't be satisfied to glean a blessing here and there, where your prayer and praise is half-hearted; come into abundant blessing. The scripture says, "The Lord under whose wings we have come to trust will recompense your work and give a full reward (Mark 10:28-30)."

Destiny and Purpose Work Together

"And as Jesus passed by, he saw a man which was blind from his birth. And his disciples asked him, saying, Master, who did sin, this man or his parents, that he was born blind? Jesus answered, neither hath this man sinned, nor his parents: but that the works of God should be made manifest in him" (John 9). This man suffered with blindness all of his life for no particular reason other than the residual effects of sin. We see examples of bad things that happen to people and simply cannot make sense of it. How can we allow the works of God to be manifested in the middle of an ugly situation?

Think of the worst thing that has happened to you in your life; if you survived then you are an overcomer. God will use your life as an example to encourage one who is about to give up. I am not suggesting that God wanted these things to happen to you. He didn't but in the course of life, we will experience adversity. The scripture reminds us that, "Man that is born of a woman is of few days and full of trouble but He shall deliver thee in six troubles: yea, in seven there shall no evil touch thee (Job 14:1, 5:19; 1 Pet. 4:1, 12)."

If the entrance of the word brings light and life with it, then the entrance of sin brings death and devastation. However, like the blind man in the example, we will face challenges on our road to destiny and we have to remember that although all things work together for our good, they are not all beneficial when they happen (Rom 8:28).

I know a young lady who moved to a different city to take a new job. It seemed like a good move, but it turned out to be a disaster. Not only did she end up without that job, it caused financial distress and she lost her home. However, during that time, she prayed and asked God to help her and to heal her.

During this time, she learned that God was not angry at her and did not need her to be so performance-minded. She ended up with a better perspective about God, His grace, and in the end, received a better job that was more of a promotion than the original job she received and she now has another home. God turned this situation around and worked it out for her good. It did not feel good during the months that she was struggling but she allowed God to help her and bring her into victory.

Judas Iscariot- Son of Perdition

Judas betrayed Jesus. Does that mean that God wanted Judas to perish? No, if the scripture says that God wishes that no man should perish but that all would come to eternal life that is exactly what God means. However, Judas did not esteem Christ for who he was and is; he remained carnal and not spiritual minded (John 17:12). He did not allow his heart to be penetrated with the good news that Jesus proclaimed or to see the kingdom of God that was preached to him day after day. His heart remained greedy and he eventually made the choice that caused him to later take his own life.

Imagine walking with a close friend for years all the while knowing that they are not truly your friend at all. Jesus knew that Judas was a betrayer from the beginning of their relationship yet he still called him friend (Ps. 41:9). It was Judas's choice to give up our Lord, but it still worked to the plan of God because Jesus was later raised from the dead after giving his life for our sins. It was unfortunate for Judas because the scripture does not say he repented but we know that God would have forgiven him.

Have you ever been betrayed by someone you cared about? Many times it is that betrayal that propels us forward toward our destiny just as Jesus' betrayal sent him to the cross. I'm sure there are examples in many of our lives that if the problem had not happened the way they did, we would still be stuck in that place and missed the greater blessing! So, let Judas kiss you. You are only responsible to show love and be forgiving. Allow yourself to move into the destiny that lies on the other side of midnight. Stop wondering and worrying about your enemies or so called friends, God is powerful enough to use them both to bless you. You have to understand that there are some individuals that don't want to bless you but they can't help themselves from blessing you. This puts to mind a story in the Old Testament of a prophet named Balaam who was asked to curse the people of Israel. He was offered lots of gold and money, but he could not. He slept on it a few days, prayed about it and in the end, the King that tried to hire him to curse God's people was furious because Balaam spoke such blessing and increase that the King wished he had never engaged the prophets help! Balaam's words were simple: "How can I curse whom God has not cursed…when He (God) has blessed I cannot revoke (Number 23:8, 24:20)."

Jesus – Our Lord

What can I say about Jesus that could do Him any justice? He is the ultimate portrait of the fulfillment of purpose and destiny. He was in all things and before all things. Christ came, in the flesh, to redeem us from the enemy. He is Emmanuel, being interpreted God with us but He still had to pray three times in the garden of Gethsemane to fulfill His destiny. He knew the agony of what He was about to go through. He prayed and sought the Father that the cup of sin and separation would pass from Him but it was His destiny.

He was destined to suffer the brutal beating that He endured, so that His cleansing blood could heal me from every disease and take away my sins (Eph.1:7). He was destined to hang on the cross and be forsaken that I might never have to be forsaken. He was willing to complete His destiny and have God the Father turn his back on Him, so that He would never have to turn his back on me. When Jesus hung on the cross and died for our sins, purpose and destiny kissed and the power of God was released on earth, to return to God what was His, mankind. Jesus was the repairer of the breach.

What is our part? He says to seek first the Kingdom of God and the other things that we desire will be ours (Matt 6:33). God will not reward us evil for good. If He promised to add to us and give us abundance, then He will. We don't have to sit around worrying and being anxious about our future. We have plenty to keep us occupied for today. There are so many things happening around us each day that can affect our lives in a negative way but that does not excuse us from giving God first place. The scripture reminds us to take no thought for tomorrow, for tomorrow shall be thought for the things of itself. Sufficient unto the day is the evil thereof (Matt. 6:34). This lets us know that nothing catches God by surprise. Some people think their situation is new to God. It's not!

God does not wring His Hands in despair or say, "oh no, what am I going to do?" How will I keep this man alive? He already knew what He was going to do. You and I must understand that God has a plan for your life and my life. You and I must connect, with Him, to know His plan for our lives. We need to remember that our Cherith always comes equipped with God's provision.

I'm here to tell you God is going to supply our every need. That includes physical, emotional or financial. When you choose to walk the path that He has chosen He is responsible and will take care of you. Jesus said in Matthew 19:29 that anyone who has left family, homes, job/vocation etc., shall inherit one-hundred fold and inherit eternal life. I interpret this to mean it will pay off in this life on earth as well as when we get to Heaven. The scriptures also tell us Jesus, although rich, became poor for our sake (2 Cor. 8:9). We also learned that he has given us the comforter, his word, the blood and his authority. We have all that we need to succeed in fulfilling his purpose for our lives. Conversely, if we chose a plan contrary to His will it leaves us open to the snares and vices of the enemy. We can see this example even in the Old Testament when God outlined the blessings of following His ways in Deuteronomy 14. Great blessing are declared for following Him, but horrible curses are outlined for those who chose against God. It is important to know that by default, and because when Adam sinned it gave Satan authority over the earth. So anytime we go against God's plan or ways we end up with what is intended for the devil – defeat and destruction (the curse).

Am I There Yet

In our quest to fulfill our purpose and walk in our destiny, we have to trust that God will meet our needs according to His riches in glory. He made a way to live in us and be one with us so he could always be with us by His Spirit. He will be our buckler and our shield. He will hide us under His shadow. I wonder what Elijah must have felt as the brook dried up right before his very eyes. I wondered if he felt abandoned or forsaken. Have you ever felt as if God has abandoned or forsaken you? And you think, God I know you told me to come here but the brook is drying up. I wondered if he felt as if God somehow let him down. Remember, the devil is the accuser of the brethren and he'll try to make you think that God has let you down. God has not forsaken you. In fact, if you're looking at a dried up brook, you are already taken care of; God cannot forget you. Hear His plan and directions then boldly take the steps He is giving you. The covenant relationship with God is stable He cannot deny Himself (you are one with Him). Like Elijah, when your brook dries up God has already constructed the provision and new channel of blessing.

We established that there are times that God will hide you because it isn't your season yet. We also see there's an assignment by God to Elijah giving him direction, insight and understanding. This resulted in him moving forward to the next place of provision and will of God. We can use Elijah's example and do the same thing because God wants to reveal our purpose and work with us to bring destiny to pass. Let's review what we have learned so far.

Points to Remember:
- *The meaning of purpose and destiny*
- *How Believers find our purpose*
- *Adversity is not our end*
- *Where purpose is there is provision*
- *There is a place of refinement*
- *Corporate purpose*
- *Individual purpose*
- *Learn the purpose of others in your life*
- *This is a journey of trust*

Chapter Eight
Is it Sin or Righteousness?

A young man and his father watched the evening news. Across the TV screen flashed images of wars, starvation, death and natural disasters. As they watched, the young man grew more anxious and distressed and he asked his father why there was so much death and destruction in the world. He said, "I mean, if there is a God in Heaven why would He let these things happen to the people that He loves?"

The father hesitated for a moment and then he replied, "Son, I don't have all the answers. I only know that God's word is true and I know that He still loves us. But let me tell you a story that may shed some light on what you see going on in this world.

You see son, when God made the world it was completely blank. His spirit moved on the face of the waters and God commanded there to be light and the light appeared. After God put everything in order, he made man and gave him dominion over all the earth. It was beautiful and peaceful; in fact, they spent a lot of time together and talked all the time. Adam, Eve and God were inseparable. But God had a sneaky, sly enemy named Satan. Eventually this enemy convinced man to disobey God which caused a separation between them. This act, which is called sin, unleashed death into the world. The consequence of sin affects man and the earth. Every person is born with this sin condition, and it causes destruction, pain, hatred and many awful things that God never intended. My son, sin is the most costly thing in the world."

The Struggle is Life

Someone asked the question is it my sin, or is it my righteousness that causes my suffering or my blessings. The answer is both. We may be persecuted for righteousness sake and we can suffer because of our own poor choices.

We may continually ask why so many unfortunate things happen to people and the lack of answers can erode our faith. We live in a sinful world and many things that happen are simply the consequences of sin being in the earth. The full redemption of the earth and the people of God have not taken place yet. Which is why we still pray "thy kingdom come thy will be done." We are still waiting for the full manifestation of His glory. There is much which remains to be seen but until then, the earth will continue to have upheaval and mankind will suffer the ravages of this world.

I would like to think that, as Christians, we could escape the pitfall of life on earth but we still reside in this natural realm. When we find ourselves in difficult situations, we need to pray and submit it to God and receive his peace.

We learn to discern His will and to trust Him while we're in that tough place. That's where the Psalmist cries out, "Yea though I walk through the valley of the shadow of death I will fear no evil. Thy rod and thy staff they comfort me (Psalm 23)" while I'm going through this dark and difficult place. In our difficult seasons, we lean on the Lord the most.

I would like to think that no believers have perished in all of the natural disasters and terrorist attacks that have taken place, but as long as we are in this world, we will still suffer natural troubles. Scripture reminds us that man, which is born of woman, is but a few days and those days are full of trouble (Job 14:1). Then it also teaches us that, He will deliver us in six troubles and in seven there shall no evil touch thee (Job 5:9). Well, which one is it. It is both, we will suffer and He will deliver but God desires that we come to the place where we trust Him enough to know that no matter what occurs in the natural, He is still God. We must remember that the sufferings of this present time are not worthy to be compared with the glory which shall be revealed in us (Rom 8:17-18). You say, "I am in God's will, so what caused this incident in my life?"

The Source of My Trouble

As stated above, it is not a sign of God's displeasure when the brook dries up; instead God has another channel of blessing already lined up. Remember, Satan is an enemy of God and man and will try to convince you and me that God is angry with us and that is the reason we are in this hard place. But remember that God will also allow our brook to dry up, so that we can move on to a new place of provision.

Typically, our response to the things of God will determine our outcomes. God is holy and expects our lives to be pleasing in His sight. Although our eternal state with God is secure because of Christ, the state of our relationship with God must also be in agreement through our actions. If we recall the story of the prodigal son, he eventually came to his senses when he found himself in a pig pen. He remembered all the blessings that he left behind. He was still a son, but he could never have received the blessing and comfort of right relationship with his father had he stayed in the pig pen. So it is in our relationship with God. We have to come to Father God in the way He has provided and that entails living the lifestyle that allows Him to bless and favor and be involved in our lives to bring the good things that He has planned.

Salvation is free but we can't remain steeped in sin and expect God's anointing to permeate our lives. If we do, we will find that we have a gospel that is preached with enticing words but without the demonstration and power of God following to give full proof of our ministry (1 Pet. 1:13-15; 2:9).

The Darkness of God

The times of darkness from God are the times of our making. It's the time to build character, spiritual muscle and increase faith levels. He wants us strong in these areas for our future reference and to meet our individual potential. During this time, it may seem as if God is not speaking or revealing, but it's a time to dig deeper into His word and seek His face... "it is the honor of Kings to search it out a matter" (Prov. 25:2)

When God allows harsh or painful conditions to afflict us, it is not to make us bitter. In difficult times we often find our strength. A lack of finances will cause you to pray about your situation. There's nothing like money to cause people to pray. When people start losing money and going broke they genuinely pray. Whenever you start having to figure out how much gas is going to cost to go across town, you know it's serious. We are mature in our faith when we can remain steadfast even when it doesn't turn out the way we planned. God already knows what we are made of but He wants us to also know. For example, Job never lost his integrity during the harshest trial of his life and we shouldn't either.

What begins to happen in us when the enemy accuses us of everything that we do wrong, we learn to fight and declare that we have no condemnation in Christ Jesus. How should one respond if there is a physical attack such as cancer, we begin to rehearse what God has says and that is "by His stripes I'm healed (Isa. 53:5)." This practice of rehearsing the word and trusting what God has said builds faith, character and spiritual strength.

Another example of being "made" during the dark times is when God led me from Memphis to Pontiac. My resources dried up and that caused me to ask God what I should do next and that started my journey from my home. I had no idea at that time that life would be better for me than it was in Memphis. God used that experience to train me how to trust Him and move by His voice and direction. Although it seemed like a dark time in my life, it is now one of my sweet memories of time with God and learning to lean on Him. God can't forget you. He says though a nursing mother forgets her child, I cannot forget you. You're the apple of My eye. God uses times of darkness when you are uncertain what is going on to move you to a new place of blessing.

The early New Testament church faced danger which forced them to move from one location to another and the gospel was spread as they traveled. They faced trials with a purpose and the purpose was to advance the kingdom of God. They learned to ask God for more boldness as persecution happened and did not pull back but moved forward to turn the world upside down with the radical commitment to the gospel. They committed to God instead of reading the persecution as a sign that God was not pleased with them.

It is said that when all else fails or when you don't know what to do, you should simply begin to worship God. He is sovereign and when we worship Him it takes us into an elevated state and changes our perspective to see things from His point of view. We begin to love Him as we see His beauty and glory and it begins to go beyond just what we want Him to do for us.

When we were the worst that we could be, Christ still died for us. What kind of love is that? Even though, He loves me, I will have setbacks and disappointments. I may suffer loss and persecution but it actually does not matter. I will continue to love Him. I will continue to obey Him and wait for His return. I will hide his word in my heart, so that I might not sin against Him (Psalm 119:11).

I don't mean to make light of our afflictions, but the word of God also states that our light afflictions cannot be compared to the glory that will be revealed in us (2 Cor. 4:17). We can endure some devilish pain in this life but God is still able to take us through every valley of the shadow of death.

The Darkness of the Enemy

The enemy of our soul draws us away from the things of God by using deception. His attack is not measured. His intent is not merely to harm but to destroy us. His seduction is slow and deliberate. He attacks our minds with fiery darts and attempts to wither our faith. Our enemy is acquainted with scripture and he knows that "all that is not of faith is sin," (Romans 14:23) so he begins his attack by telling us that what God says is not true. If he can get us to agree with his lies, then he can oppress us with his darkness through confusion.

He presents evidence that is contrary to scripture and then he waits for us to come into an agreement with it. Since he cannot curse what God has blessed he has to get us to curse ourselves with our mouths. He uses our power against us because he knows that life and death are in the power of the tongue. Once weakened, he will entice us further into whatever sin or temptations that is from our past. Although drawn away by our own lust the enemy presents the package. He knows our temptations.

Once the darkness of the enemy has full course in your life, you will find that you are compelled to sin and are no longer in control of your life. Once his hook is in your jaw, he will expose you for all to see. I think that is why Jesus said, "the prince of this world comes but he has nothing in me" Jesus' only desire was to please the Father, so the enemy could not tempt Him. When there is a desire in our hearts that is not aligned with God's heart we have to get it out.

God's Judgment is on Sin

The wages of sin is still death. Sin and hell are two subjects that are not discussed very much anymore. They are unpleasant topics and I would rather avoid them also but truth must be told. The truth is that the scripture warns that if we practice sin (this means that we habitually continue in sinful behavior until it becomes our way of life.) we are like a dog that has gone back to its own vomit. The penalty is already set for sin and if we would like to avoid the penalty, we must avoid the sin.

God is not sitting around waiting for man to fall. He does not enjoy watching His children get themselves into predicaments which crucify Christ again. God wants us to put our bodies under subjection and renew our minds. He will not judge us while we are attempting to break free of our issues. He gives us grace and His mercies are new every day. But if we have decided that we are just going to continue in sin because we like it and it feels good then that we must know eventually we will experience the consequences of our decision. God will speak to us concerning our sin and warn us several times before we encounter His judgment.

God is gracious and slow to anger (Ps. 103:8). Some have decided that God should understand their desires and excuse them. But the scripture is the same for everyone, "God is no respecter of persons" (Rom. 2:11). What He requires for one, He does for another. What He will do for one, He will do for another. It is best to stop our ungodly practices before we are judged. You have seen it on the news, as some solider in God's army is exposed for their sins. It is a sad sight, as we watch powerful men and women of God stripped by the enemy and paraded around. It is the equivalent of being naked for the world to see. Warning! If the enemy sees that he can eliminate one, he will certainly try for another.

Because of My Goodness

On the opposite end of the spectrum, from the belief that we always suffer because of our sin, are those who believe that they are blessed because they are so righteous. They think that they should receive more from the Lord than others based on their own goodness. The story Jesus tells in Matt. 20:1-16 is an excellent illustration of this. All the workers were paid the same amount. Those who started work first envied their brothers because they felt they should have received more simply because they began working earlier. Please remember, it was not their money to give and it was not their work. God blessed all of them with the same amount. If our righteousness is like filthy rags, we can never earn the status of being right unless we are in Christ. He is our righteousness and the payment for our sins.

However, there are benefits to walking in obedience to the word of God. As we walk in obedience on one level, God will promote us to another level. There is a standard of holiness. We should not live as if we don't know the truth. If we know what is right and we don't do it, it is counted against us as sin. If we live righteously, we will not have to suffer many of the problems that accompany a life of sin.

I knew a lady who believed Jesus for her salvation. After a while, she started wearing her dresses down to her ankles and stopped wearing make-up and fixing her hair because she thought that neglecting her appearance was evidence of her holiness. Her outward appearance had nothing to do with her righteousness. She also lost her compassion and she began to think that she was righteous all by herself. She became self-righteous. Then she took a hard fall. But it was during that time, she realized that God still loved her and it was His love that kept drawing her out of her situation. She finally understood that Jesus is her righteousness. It was His love that gave her abundant grace and His gift of righteousness (Rom. 5:17).

God Forgives Sin

Yes! God does forgive us but we may still suffer the consequences of our sin. A friend of mine tells the story of his salvation experience where ever he goes. His marriage was in trouble and he had an affair but he desperately wanted to change. Someone took him to a little church on Long Island. It was a Sunday night in June and a warm breeze was blowing as the moon was shining into the small sanctuary. The pastor was at the door greeting each person as they came for evening service. My friend did not know that his life was about to be changed forever. He did not know that he would encounter the power of Jesus Christ that night.

My friend went into the sanctuary and the pastor pointed toward him over his thick wire framed glasses and said. "You sir, may I pray for you?" My friend was shocked, he hesitated but he eventually went to the front of the sanctuary. The pastor began to tell him everything that was going on in his life and he said that he was amazed. Then the man of God placed his hand on my friend's forehead and he fell to the floor by the power of God. He became conscious of a strong presence of love that seemed to penetrate his heart. He stood up and staggered to his seat and he wondered what happened. He believed that what he experienced were for those who "had religion," and for those who already believed and he did not. What he didn't realize is that God has the power to touch whomever He wants. My friend gave his heart to the Lord that day. He repented and God forgave him and now he preaches the gospel with power. Unfortunately, his marriage did not survive the mistakes of his past.

The Grace of God

One of the definitions of grace is the unmerited favor of God. It is our pardon and the kindness of Christ in His ultimate sacrifice that He procured atonement for man. Someone has defined atonement as "at-one-ment" we become one with God. Christ is our bridge to the Father. He mends the breach that was originally made in the garden. Once again, our predicaments may not have anything to do with our righteousness or sin. It may simply be a matter of life's circumstances. What we must remember is that we have new mercy each day. I want mercy and I love the grace of God. His grace grows sweeter and sweeter as the days go by. The more I get to know Him; I realize how much He loves me. The scripture teaches us that on my best days, when I have done no wrong, when I have fasted all day and night, it is still as filthy rags. All of our righteousness apart from Jesus is like filthy rags. God's grace is the only payment which can entirely cover the cost of sin. His grace is truly sufficient for all that we will encounter.

The question is have we received His grace. Have you accepted the payment for your sins that was made by Christ on the hill of Golgotha? All that is required is that we receive it. As we accept His grace, we will begin to see His glory. When the glory of God is operating, we are able to stand in our furnace and face our detractors with confidence that God is on our side. His grace extends our ability to go through our situations and continue to offer the sacrifice of praise. And we recognize that even if He does not show up on our schedule He is still God. Jesus and Paul prayed three times for their situations to change but the sovereignty of God prevailed and they accepted His perfect will.

Even in our corporate worship, when we receive His grace, the Holy Spirit will take over and the presence of God will blanket the service until no one can stand up to minister. When we make our agenda secondary to God's agenda and worship the Lord in spirit and in truth, we will experience the grace and glory of God. It does not take God all day to do anything. If we could just get out of the way and allow God to have his way. Then we will see the power of God released, yokes destroyed and souls saved. Grace is the most valuable gift in the world.

Points to Remember:

- *We live in a fallen world*
- *Sin is costly*
- *There is darkness from God*
- *There is darkness from the enemy*
- *There is a blessing in obedience*
- *Christ is our righteousness*
- *Judgment remains on sin*
- *God forgives sin*
- *Grace is the ultimate gift*

Chapter Nine
Raising Your Level of Expectation, Times and Seasons

"It is said an Eastern monarch once charged his wise men to invent him a sentence to be ever in view which should be true and appropriate in all times and situations. They presented him the words: 'And this too, shall pass away.' How much it expresses, how chastening in the hour of pride, how consoling in the depths of affliction!" - Abraham Lincoln

What is Time?

We serve a God who's already alive in our tomorrow. You and I are limited by time, God is not. He stepped out of time that is why we call Him the Alpha and the Omega, the beginning and the end. He knows the end of a thing at the beginning. We are preoccupied with the passing of time; and the ways in which we utilize and manage our time. If time were a commodity, I am confident we would buy more of it. We have various methods of measuring time which we can assign a value to even the smallest measurement. The list looks something like this: eons – an indefinitely long time, at least two or more eras, or one billion years, eras, ages, centuries, years, seasons, months, weeks, days, hours, minutes, seconds, nanoseconds, picoseconds, millisecond and microseconds. And, with all of these measurements of time we still divide them further into zones on the earth, so that it is already tomorrow somewhere on the planet.

Time is a system of measurement that God has given man to assist us in governing our lives. God lives outside of time in eternity; therefore, He has no need of time. To Him, one day is like a thousand years a thousand years are like a day. In other words, time is irrelevant!

Time measures events on a continuum, based on what we deem to be past, present, or future. Our lives are based on time. A baby is born and grows into a child. The child develops into an adult and becomes a man. The man matures, ages eventually he dies (James 4:14). All of these events are marked by time.

Time is one of the foundational systems of man's limited knowledge. As far as we know there is no place on earth that exists outside of time. To define time leads to a vast array of explanations. One explanation, which describes our perception of time, is this:

"Time is a component of the measuring system used to sequence events, to compare the durations of events and the intervals between them to quantify the motions of objects. Time has been a major subject of religion, philosophy, science but defining it in a non-controversial manner applicable to all fields of study has consistently eluded the greatest scholars" –Wiki

The Search for Answers

In his book, *The Time Machine*, H. G. Wells tells the story of a man who invents a time machine to return to the past and save his fiancée from her death. He returns to the time just before her tragic death. He is able to change some of the events eventually his fiancée still dies on the same day.

To find out why he was not able to change the outcome of events, he travels to the future. He is certain they already have the answers to time travel. His first encounter is with a society whose motto is, "The future is now," but they still do not possess the answers to his questions.

The young professor travels another seven years into the future and finds that society has destroyed itself by exploding devices on the moon. As the moon disintegrates, it hits the earth and propels his machine many years forward in time. At last, he encounters a society that has deteriorated into cannibalism all remnants of modern life are gone. The young man finally realizes that no matter how many times he travels to the past; he can never change what happen. We simply don't have all the answers.

Our life's journey can be like a time machine. It can propel us to strange new environments in a moment's notice. We can be going ahead in our existence suddenly we are interrupted by life altering conditions. Like the traveler in Well's novel, we have to adjust. It doesn't matter if the situation is a positive or negative one; we still have to take a moment and make the necessary adjustments. However, unlike the traveler in Well's novel, our ability to rebound from difficult situations rests solely on our foundation. If we are established on the solid foundation of Christ, we have the ability to recover from any situation. The scripture lets us know that we are more than conquerors.

One of the most crucial aspects of life is being able to ascertain the days and seasons you are in or are approaching. When we comprehend the times and seasons we are in, we are also able to enjoy times of peace and prosperity without fear of the future. I know it goes against some of our current theology, but along with joy, we will receive some trouble in this life.

When we know God's timing, we will be able to accept the inevitable challenges we will face. How do I know this? I only know what the scripture says, in Ecclesiastes 3:1-8. In this text, King Solomon offered his wisdom on the phases of human existence.

But, even with all of the changes in life, we must remember that God is constant. He is not going to change on you. Jobs may change, ministries may fluctuate, our economic stability may falter, even our health may suffer challenges we can always rely on the immutability of God's guidance (Heb. 6:17-19). Don't let your soul be cast down because of a difficult season. Hold your head up and remember that you are only as strong as your foundation. Who is your foundation?

Discerning the Times

The scripture speaks of: due time, set times, the fullness of time, sundry times, end times, the watches of the Lord. We are even cautioned to redeem the time. The Lord gives us the ability to recognize the times and seasons by His Holy Spirit (1 Cor. 2:9-10). The Spirit of God leads us into all truth, He is our guide and our teacher (Jn. 16:13). God has always given men the ability to discern the times and seasons. "And of the children of Issachar, which were men that had an understanding of the times, to know what Israel ought to do; the head of them were two hundred; and all their brethren were at their commandment (1 Chron.12:32)."

The sons of Issachar are given notable mention in Scripture because they, from among Israel's twelve tribes, understood the time and discerned what God was doing by bringing David to the throne as His anointed. Discernment of God's times and seasons are necessary in order to cooperate with God in purposeful action and to embrace and sustain a God-given hope during times of change.

When we are in touch with the Spirit of God, we will be able to cooperate with His agenda and not go past the road signs the Lord gives us. There are times when we need to accept the changes we encounter; there are other times when we need to fight. Only when we seek God will we know the difference. There are also seasons and times in our life that we can't figure out what God is doing, at those times we just work with God.

Joseph had a revelation of times and seasons through his dreams. He was able to know the will of God for his future because of his dreams. There were many situations on the way to the fulfillment of his destiny it appeared that his dreams would never materialize. It wasn't until he had suffered and been wrongly accused that the timing and purpose of God was accomplished (Gen. 37:1).

Joseph also had the ability to interpret dreams, which he did for Pharaoh and secured the future of a nation (Gen. 47:6). God still does this with his children today. He will often give us a glimpse of the final product. He will allow us to see where he is taking us but on the way, like the lens of a camera, everything seems to fade to black and nothing looks like what God showed you. You know what He said, concerning a certain thing, but suddenly your vision is not clear. Like the film in the camera, we have to be processed in the solutions of God which helps us to develop into the photograph that He desires.

Daniel also had a revelation of the times and seasons through his dreams and interpretation and he made the will of God known to King Nebuchadnezzar concerning what would happen in later days. It was said that Daniel had an excellent spirit and the scripture tells us that, "God gave Daniel and the other Hebrew boys, knowledge and skill in all learning and wisdom; and Daniel had an understanding in all visions and dreams (Dan. 2:28-30)."

Daniel ministered before the king. His gifts made room for him and brought him before great men (Dan. 2:48-49). If God is no respecter of persons, then he can give you wisdom and knowledge. He can give you the gift of dreams and interpretations. Get close to God and ask Him for the gifts that He wants you to have. It is the one thing that God allows us to covet. He says we're to covet the best gifts.

You are an Eternal Being

Because we existed in the mind of God before the foundation of the world, our spirit is eternal and is not confined by time (Eph. 1:2-4). Although, the spirit and soul are privileged to the working of time they are not restricted by it. God has our times in His hand, He has given us this temporal body to assist us in this time intensive existence, and spiritually we are seated in heavenly places with Christ. Our temporal bodies will one day be changed and raised incorruptible and immortal (1 Cor.15:51-53).

In our current state, the only means of transcending time is through prayer. So, it is our spirit man that has the freedom of movement from one realm to another. The Apostle Paul shares his experience of being in a trance (2 Cor. 12:1-7). In the trance, he appears to be more conscious of the spiritual realm than the physical realm (Acts 22:17). While he is in this trance, he travels to the third heaven where he is given revelations in abundance. The scripture does not say exactly, but I believe that Paul was in prayer when he had this experience. How did he travel? His spirit man traveled through the heavens and came to rest in a place of immense revelations. This incident gave Paul the ability to endure the hardships he would face in ministry (Acts 17:23-30).

On the isle of Patmos, the beloved Apostle John says, "I was in the Spirit on the Lord's day and heard behind me a great voice as of a trumpet", John not only hears what the voice is saying he begins to see a vision which is recorded in scripture in the book of Revelation. These are two examples of men of God who had given themselves to the ministry of prayer to the point that they were both given unusual revelations for the benefit of their ministries and the edification of the church. But those were apostles, not people like me, you say.

Well, God is not going to give us any extra Biblical revelations. He will give us revelations that can help our ministry and edify the body of Christ. He will not only tell you what to do, He will give you specific instructions on the methods you need to employ to achieve your goals. He is concerned about our everyday matters. God wants us to come into a place where we depend on Him and Him alone.

When we can come to the place where we trust Him and Him alone we have come to a great level of growth. It takes growth for us to come to the place where we're no longer depending on our education or jobs for our future. The average individual will only stay on a job for seven years. And so we've got to learn to depend more and more on the Lord. God wants us to come to a place where we don't trust in the arms of flesh regardless of whose arm it is. The Bible says some men trust in chariots and some men trust in horses, He wants us to come to the place where we don't trust in the flesh.

In the 60's and 70's, there was no such thing as outsourcing or downsizing. You found a job you stayed there for life. Times have changed. We are in a time when people are being replaced by robots and jobs are outsourced to foreign countries. It causes us to depend on the Lord.

The God Spot

There is a place where God wants to have in your life and no one else can have it. He doesn't want your job or your spouse in that spot. He doesn't want that new baby boy or that new baby girl in that spot. It is God's spot. If you keep Him in His spot He will lift you up. When I was a child, my daddy had a particular spot at the dinner table. We just didn't sit wherever we wanted to sit, if we did, we got up from that spot when daddy came home.

Does Jesus have a spot in your life? Does He have a place that no one else can take? If He doesn't, clear out the clutter and give Him some of your valuable time. Once you do, you will be able to receive a great revelation about finally starting the ministry God gave you. I will go further and say that there should be a place in your house that's just for God, a place where you go to meet with Him.

It will become the place where He may give you the next step in your career, or reveal the intents of your heart. Although, we are eternal beings we live in these physical bodies and only have a certain amount of time to accomplish our life's work. When we meet the Lord, we want to hear well done, good and faithful servant. God is not a God of happenstance. So, find your God spot and get deliberately busy with the things of God.

Missing It

When we miss God's timing we have to wait until the season returns. I recall the story of Paul, who received instruction from the Lord not to sail because they were sailing into a storm. As a prisoner, Paul had no control over the journey he warned his jailers of the dangers ahead. The soldiers didn't believe Paul and they chose to ignore him. They deliberately sailed and ran into much difficulty.

Paul received a second instruction from the Lord to have everyone stay with the ship and there would be no loss of life. Needless to say, the soldiers paid attention to Paul's words this time. They ran aground just as the Lord said. Some were swimming, some came in on boards, some on broken pieces, and God was faithful to get them to their final destination. (Acts 27:9-30)

Their disobedience brought unnecessary suffering for all. Can you imagine the fear of the men on the boat with Paul, as they rowed against the storm to no avail? They probably thought they were going to die. They suffered for days. They were trapped on a violent sea, in darkness and held on as the ship broke into pieces. Have you ever been trapped anywhere for any length of time? I think it would be dreadful. I also think it would turn you into a prayer warrior just like it did for the men with Paul. They sailed out of God's timing. If we are sensitive to the leading of the Holy Spirit, we will not miss God's timing.

There are situations that appear to happen out of God's timing. They are situations that you never expected. I remember when my wife died. I'd been married for twenty-five years; I had to live one day at a time. Every day I would walk down Squirrel Road then I would walk down Tienken Road to Squirrel Road. I'd stand there and pray. I said "Lord if you would just let me make it to lunch time" then when I'd get past lunch, I'd say "Lord if you would just give me enough grace to make it to dinner." And then as time progressed, I said "Lord if you would just let me go to sleep tonight." Each day I had to depend on Him to get to the next day.

Jesus wants us to walk like that every day; not just when tragedy happens. One day at a time, He wants us to say, "God I need your help for today." That's why it says morning by morning new mercies will arise. No matter what you're going through today, if you can just hold out to 11:59, because at midnight, God's going to download a fresh load of grace for you. He reminds us that His grace is sufficient; we are made perfect whenever we get weak because when we get weak, we begin to see ourselves as weak and we become strong because a glorious exchange with God is made. He gives us His strength for our weakness. Glory to God!

The Right Place at the Right Time

Elijah, the prophet, was at a specific place. And that was the only place that he could be and be right with God. If he had gone anywhere else, he would have starved to death because God had provisions for him at a certain place. When we are in the right place at the right time, we will have a sense of fulfillment. That is not to say that it will not come with challenges. Again, remember that the scripture reminds us that, within the doors of opportunity, there are many adversaries (1 Cor. 16:9).

We sometimes have the idea that God only give us nice assignments. If it is too difficult we begin to question if it is God. When He sends us to a hard place we are supposed to stay there, not complaining realizing that He knows just what we need in order to get us into shape.

Don't run from the difficult place. He put you there. It is preparation for your ultimate assignment, where you will finally occupy the right place at the right time. When time and place coincide, we are able to accomplish God's purpose with greater ease because God's grace will help us. Remember, success is the outcome of being prepared and at the right place, at the right time. We would do well to discern the timing of God; because it carries the weight of the power of God behind it.

The scripture tells us of a day when the sun stood still. God will recalibrate time for you as He did for Joshua (Jos.11). As Joshua fought against the Amorites, he prayed for a miracle and God made the sun and the moon hold their positions until the people had vengeance on their enemies. King Hezekiah lay sick and dying; when the prophet Isaiah came to tell him of his impending death the king prayed and God granted him fifteen years (2 Kings 20:1-11). Hezekiah asked for a sign of his healing, God turned the sun dial back ten degrees.

Time is a small thing for God. One element that is evident in both of these examples is the power of prayer. Prayer transcends time, it is the only way we can redeem time or adjust time for our benefit. Finally, the Apostle Paul, in the book of Acts, reminds us that God determines our times and the bounds of our habitation (Acts 17:26).

I knew of a dear couple who were called into the ministry. They were offered a church building by their pastor, who was willing to help them establish the ministry. The church building was paid for; it also had a semi-professional musician and many members who wanted the couple to take over the church. The couple decided not to take it, another couple ended up taking the church.

Since that time, the couple has been waiting to begin the church that God called them to establish. They have remained in an uncomfortable predicament for several years while God works His will out in them. They often wonder if they missed God's timing concerning the church they were offered. I am certain that one day they will have a thriving church where they will be helpful to others who are trying to discern God's timing.

Inventory

At the end of every year, many of us sit down and take inventory. We examine our goals to see if we have accomplished the things that we have purposed in our hearts. It is an opportune time to scrutinize our relationships, to take a look at our habits, and to establish some new objectives. It is time to ask ourselves a few questions about times and seasons. Is there something right now that you need God to put on hold or accelerate for your benefit? Do you think you are in God's timing, or have you been distracted or deliberately missed the timing of the Lord because you have determined your own agenda?

It is only when we are in God's timing that we can raise our level of expectation to achieve the desired results. Why? Because the power of God will lead us forward and assist us to accomplish our task. He wants us to be successful. We can't change the past. We can only move in God's timing starting today. We can commit to being sensitive to the leading of the Lord and obey His will over our own. We have to remind ourselves that God still works miracles never allow fear to stop us.

Some of the things we have learned in this chapter: This is a lesson of Cherith. God's servant must come to the place where they trust God alone; you must trust Him just like the song, "Absolutely". God will bring you to a place where you trust Him unconditionally. There won't be any doubt in your mind and no doubt in God's mind that you are trusting in Him and Him alone. God is in control of our lives. It's not the devil, it's not circumstances. God is in control and that is why we make our appeal to Him. The scripture reminds us that He is both the Author and Finisher of our faith (Heb. 12:2). He is sovereign.

Points to Remember:

- *Man is preoccupied with time*
- *God has a purpose for time*
- *God determines our habitations*
- *Spirit is eternal*
- *Prayer transcends time*

Chapter Ten
The Finishing Anointing

The Road Not Taken **by Robert Frost**

Two roads diverged in a yellow wood
And sorry I could not travel both
And be one traveler, long I stood
And looked down one as far as I could

To where it bent in the undergrowth;
Then took the other, as just as fair,
And having perhaps the better claim,
Because it was grassy and wanted wear;

Though as for that, the passing there
Had worn them really about the same,
And both that morning equally lay
In leaves no step had trodden black.

Oh, I kept the first for another day!
Yet knowing how way leads on to way,

> I doubted if I should ever come back.
>
> I shall be telling this with a sigh
>
> Somewhere ages and ages hence:
>
> Two roads diverged in a wood and I –
>
> I took the one less traveled by,
>
> And that has made all the difference.

The Wayfarers

There are many roads but only one leads to truth. As the scripture reminds us, "There is a way that seems right but the end thereof are death (Prov. 16:25)." As believers we are charged to find the road that leads to truth and stay on it (Matt.7:13-14). There are many childhood fables of unequal opponents, which illustrate moral lessons.

The nuance of the narratives is, it is not the one that is the fastest at the beginning of the race, it is the one who is diligent that wins. Our walk as believers is often characterized like a race. In our race, we must stay on course we must learn to navigate the terrain. As the scripture reminds us, the race is not given to the swift, nor to the strong, but to those who endure to the end. It is common knowledge that, in a relay race, the fastest runner is placed in the last leg of the race. He is called the anchor.

The anchor runner determines what is needed to win the race. The anchor is anointed to finish. Their ability is a result of training and deliberate action. The Holy Spirit is the source of our anointing. But we also have to apply ourselves to the principles of scripture by intentional action, when we do; we will grow in the grace and knowledge of God and have active participation with the Holy Spirit to stir our anointing.

God will complete the work he began in us; He has given us an anointing to finish our assignments. What is the anointing? To anoint is to smear, rub over, or set apart for a specific function or office just as kings were anointed for office. When we are anointed, we possess the ability to do a certain task. We are endowed, with the power, to accomplish our God-assigned goal. Just as Jesus was anointed by the Holy Spirit He went about doing good and healing all those who were oppressed by the enemy (Acts 10:38).

We have the same spirit within us to accomplish even greater works. We find the purpose of the anointing in Luke 4:18. The anointing is given to preach the gospel, to heal the brokenhearted, to preach deliverance to the captives, the recovery of sight to the blind, to set at liberty them that are bruised. As believers, we share the ministry of Jesus (2 Cor. 1:21-22). The spirit that anointed Jesus for His ministry is birthed on the inside of the believer when he is born again. It is the same spirit that raised Jesus from the dead. It is the same Holy Spirit that the Apostles walked in, so that even their shadow was able to heal the sick. He, the Holy Spirit, is our guide and our teacher (1 Jn. 2:27). When we are anointed, we will have a better understanding of scripture as the Spirit of God illuminates our mind, so that we are no longer ignorant of His truth. We will appreciate the simplicity of the gospel. The gospel is simple; at least God intended it to be simple (2 Cor.11:3).

It is time to Rule

You have just come out of the wilderness you know why you have been anointed. You understand your unique function. The attributes that we utilize in the wilderness gives us the ability to have a finishing anointing. You need a revelation of dominion or authority to operate in the finishing anointing. Our understanding of dominion gives us the ability to complete our assignment. To have dominion is to possess the ability to rule. It gives us control or the power to complete.

On our journey, we encounter obstacles that are assigned to derail us, to prevent us from completing our assignment. Typically it is something that you have encountered before, so you should not be surprised. The packaging may change but the test will be the same. Now, according to your experiences, you are able to confront your adversary with the spiritual weapons you have acquired. And you dominate your surroundings because God is in operation inside of you. We have the combination that brings about dominion.

We understand that our faith, our praise our application of wisdom will allow us to have dominion in our situations. Faith, our belief system, is our foundation. When we develop a strong foundation you can erect a fairly large building on top of it because it can carry the weight. Faith is our launching pad. It is the basis of our great ideas and our persistent hope. We are finishing our journey on a promise. Faith is a promise because we do not yet see the manifestation of what we desire. But the one who promised is faithful. The good thing is that when we are working for God, we don't have to worry if we will be treated fairly because we know that He will exceed our expectations.

Praise inspires us to continue regardless of the circumstances. We praise God because we have prior experience with overcoming the tactics of the adversary to derail our progress. We have also come to the understanding that we don't need to fight every battle. God being alive in our praise strengthens us as we praise Him, so that we may persevere during our struggles. While we are praising God, He is working things out in our favor, so that we are able to hold our peace and allow the Lord to fight our battles. As in the scripture, our praise confounds the enemy.

Wisdom, in operation, imparts the knowledge to circumvent the difficulties we encounter along the way. Wisdom keeps us on the journey. When we are distracted, wisdom will not let us totally lose sight of our goal. Wisdom gives us the ability to select our battles and recognize the weakness of the enemy. Wisdom imparts strategies to accomplish the purpose for which we have been anointed. Wisdom helps us make up our minds to follow God, rather than man. And we know that God is going to be with us even if the brook dries up. We will still be here because God has sent us here. It is a settled issue. We don't have a war going on in our minds. We are not double-minded because we're not following man we're following the true and living God.

The Journey

We are travelers on a journey, each of us with a special function; our destination is assured if we continue on the road. We are wayfarers. What is a wayfarer? The wayfarer is a traveler. The entire course is not revealed to a wayfarer. This journey is traveled by faith. As New Testament believers, we have the advantage of the Holy Spirit on the inside of us. He is our guide during the journey and He grants us insight to the areas on the road that we cannot see with our natural eyes.

What are you attempting to complete? The scripture reminds us to be not weary in well doing for in due season you will reap if you faint not. The obstacles you encounter along the way are designed to make you quit and throw in the towel, but we are running our race to receive the prize. So we run that we might obtain. We are finishers. We no longer vacillate between two opinions. We have decided to run with the Lord and stay the course regardless of the cost. We strive lawfully for masteries because we want a crown. We have dominion.

When Will I Finish?

Will we ever truly be finished? Well, yes and no. As believers, we may finish certain tasks that we are given but we are never finished as long as we are in these physical bodies. We are always in what I call process. In the process, we are being perfected by the various challenges we face. If we could be processed in private it would be ideal, that way everyone would not be privy to our shortcomings. But God is more concerned with building character than making us comfortable.

It is only when we are no longer in this earthly body that we will have completed our divine assignment. God will have completed His work in us. Each of us only has a certain amount of time to accomplish our goals. Until that time, we have many assignments along the way which we will have the opportunity to bring to fruition. So, in the total scheme of things we are bound by the laws of the universe, one day we have to leave this physical body which is deteriorating and put on an incorruptible body more suited to the next realm. We will be finished with our work on earth but will live eternally.

Identifying My Gifts

Do you operate in your gifts, or are you focused on your shortcomings? If you spend all of your time preoccupied with your deficiencies, you will never hone your skills. What do you do well? What can you do like no one else? It is God's idea to perfect your gifts to reassure you that it is His desire for you to share them with others. Finishers are familiar with their abilities and use them to their advantage to bless others.

I have a friend who wanted to go back to school and get his college degree. He knew that he had gifts and abilities that were lying dormant; he wanted finally to put them to proper use. In fact, he intended to begin a new career utilizing his untapped gifts; he wanted to finish what he started so many years before. He counted the cost, worried that it would affect his family negatively. He found that his sense of accomplishment in fulfilling his destiny outweighed the small inconveniences that he and his family endured. After school, he quit his old job and now has the career he always wanted.

The Importance of Place

We see that Cherith was a specific place it was the only place that Elijah could be and be right with God. God puts us in a certain place. He was in the place exactly where God wanted him to be. If he'd have gone anywhere else, he would have starved to death. God ordered provision for Elijah He ordered them to deliver it to the brook Cherith.

When the Lord sends you into a difficult place, there can be a tendency to want to be somewhere else. For example, when God sends a person into your life who gets on your nerves, it's easy to question God's intentions. You say, God is it them or me? Here God was saying, He put us in a place, it's a place of struggle. You are like a butterfly.

The butterfly, a caterpillar before it's transformed into a butterfly, has to break out of the struggle. And the struggling process of tearing out the cocoon is the precise thing that helps them survive once they get out. If you and I cut the cocoon, then the butterfly will die.

God is putting you and me in struggles that will make us ready for the next situation that we're going to face, because it makes us stronger. It's part of the preparation process. And what we must do is to learn that if God sends us to Cherith that He knows what He's doing. It's a trust issue. If God sent me here, He knew what it was going to be like before I got here, then I've got to trust God in the midst of this process.

Wherever you are, if God led you there, then He wants you there and it's a trust issue. The only place for us to be is the place where God sends us. If we find ourselves in difficult situations, the best thing we can do is submit to it as the will of God for your life and learn to trust Him while we are there. If you're led by God and you are in a difficult situation, you've got to believe that God led you there and every day you have to ask Him for grace.

When my wife died I would say God give me grace for today. I didn't ask for the anointing. I didn't ask for financial breakthrough. I had to confess over and over, Lord I trust You! Lord I trust You every day. So God will allow us to experience difficulties, so we can confess the Lord. No, I don't understand all of this I know to trust You. Do you trust Him?

Renewed Vision

Finishers have a vision! You can never achieve that which you cannot conceive in your mind. You must be able to see it. How can you create a particular result if you don't know what it looks like? What is it that you are trying to create? What will it do? What will it cost to bring it to fruition? Oh, yes! There is always a cost for the mission. I know that you have heard it before it is best to write the vision and give yourself a deadline for completion.

Write the vision and make it clear, so that those who see it will be able to run with it. You may not complete it on the assigned date I am certain that you won't be far behind your deadline. Writing things down is one of the ways that you will begin to understand how truly invested you are in the vision. As you write you will get more ideas then develop the details of what you are attempting. As one writer put it, "How can I know what I think, until I see what I have to say?"

Kairos

Finishers seize the moment! Because they have the advantage of being familiar with their gifts and abilities, the finisher puts their talents and abilities to work creating the vision they have developed. They will have the experience to follow through when an opportunity presents itself. The moment of immense crisis or opportunity is called *Kairos* in the Greek. It is a time that is critical for our advancement. It is the moment when time, training, and opportunity meet to propel you into another dimension.

The *Kairos* moment usually takes you to a level where you have never been. You may find yourself in settings that are unfamiliar to you; you may be feeling unqualified for your new assignments. Don't worry about it, you are ready. You have been preparing for this moment all along. God is implementing His plan for you. You may find yourself sitting in boardrooms with political leaders, or you may be asked to participate in organizations that connect you to networks that have the resources you need for your new projects. You are being positioned for the commanded blessing.

Deliberate Success

Finishers are deliberate, they schedule their success. You truly cannot accomplish much haphazardly. I know because I have tried. You will spin your wheels without any quantifiable success. The things you achieve will be hit and miss, until you are no longer hit and miss.

One of the things a well-known author mentions during his many speaking engagements is his writing schedule. He does not have anyone standing over him, so he has to be his own motivation he attributes to his success, the completion of several award winning novels, to his deliberate writing schedule. I remember the story of another famous writer, who sold all his possessions, to maintain his home while he finished his novel. He became one of the most celebrated novelists of the 20th century because he decided to finish what he started. We have to determine to be self-starters and finishers, while simultaneously being able to identify the end of our mission.

Know Your Anointing

Some of us have the ability to recognize the gifts and talents of others. If you have this ability, you should be able to put together effective teams. Some people have brilliant ideas, this does not mean they are the person to implement them; other people are trouble shooters. They know how to come in and straighten things out without destroying the entire program; once they have restored order they are finished. Some people are initiators, they have the ability to begin a work and position the appropriate people, and it is not their anointing to carry the burden of the project. Don't get the impression that these people are not finishers because they don't see the work to the end; that is not their calling.

Some are anointed with the gift of teaching they have the ability to dissect a subject to its core components. In fact, we are in the era of the teachers however, everyone is not a teacher. I knew a preacher, who was an evangelist to his family, they felt that teaching was more dignified, they influenced him to stop preaching and to settle down so that he could teach. He lost his anointing trying to please a man and not God. If you take on a mantle that does not fit, it will only delay your true purpose and destiny. David did not want King Saul's armor and shield to go out and fight the giant Goliath. David wanted to use that which was familiar. He knew what he could do. He understood his anointing. Walk in what you know about yourself and others. We are finishers.

When God took Elijah to boot camp it was all part of him being trained as a prophet. Remember I told you earlier He's taking him from just being a man of God, to becoming God's mouthpiece. Touch your mouth right now and say this is God's mouth. God has you in certain situations and circumstances for you to become His mouthpiece. Oh yes, when you go into the trenches with someone you are able to speak for them. Once you've gone through a battle with someone you know how they feel because you are in the foxhole together.

God was building a man of God. He knew that in order for Elijah to stand in power on Mt. Carmel, he must first be broken at the Cherith. God says, "I see you are at the brook, I know later on I'm going to have you on Mt. Carmel where you're going to take on the 450 false prophets, and you will be calling down fire from Heaven. But before you begin to call down the fire from Heaven, I have seen how you respond when the brook dries up. I want to see if you are a fair weather Christian, I want see if you're still going to be the same, so I have to take you to hard places." I received a prophetic word from Bishop Hamon he said, "The one thing I have placed in you Joyce is the ability to stand."

It may look like you made the wrong decision but I release the tenacity and stability to be unmovable in adversity. We have the same goal in our lives today. Many of us have attended the same university that Elijah attended. We are the alumni of Dry Brook University. Has anyone been beside the dry brook before? God, this thing has dried up. Don't worry about it, those of you who are attending, there are some other individuals that are enrolling. Brooks are beginning to dry up in your life, you will not break rank even when bombs are going off all around you.

Find a group that will not lose focus in battle. Find the group that is holding their position. We all have a position in this relay race toward purpose. We want to be able to repeat the sentiments of the Apostle Paul and say that we have run our race and have completed our course. Please remember that we are wayfarers. We don't have the entire course mapped out for us. The One we rely on is faithful and will perfect that which concerns us. We are encouraged to run our race with patience (Heb.12:1).

To run with patience and complete the course, we have to activate our faith and know without a doubt that we are in God's will. When we know we are in His will, we will become sensitive to the voice of God. We will have an ear to hear and follow His divine direction, as we learn to understand His times and seasons. All of this leads us to deepen our relationship with the Lord. When we purpose in our hearts to finish our course, we will have the grace to accept our purpose and destiny to move by assignment depending on God's commanded blessing to sustain us while we are hidden according to His design. We will stay on the wall, like the worshiping warriors before us, until we are finished.

God has said our church has a "finishing anointing". Anyone that has spent time with me in the house of God received instruction and been through the process know when I release them, they have the ability to stand because they know how to war a vigorous warfare. They can say for God I live and die. There are some individuals who know how to start. But God has given us not only the ability to start but to finish this thing. I won't quit until He says well done. I'm not going to stop because the brook dries up.

My advice today is to come to a place early where you roll everything over to the Lord and trust Him to take care of you. He's got more for you than you think. We are building momentum. We aren't slowing down, we are picking up speed. We are almost at the finish line. We're about to finish this thing. Some people know how to start a thing glory to God; there are some other individuals who know how to close it out. We know not to quit. We know how to close out. We are finishers. Victory is in the air we have made up our minds. We have come to take the spoils. I'm coming out victorious. We're not only going to see the Promised Land, we're going to possess it. We're going to embrace it. We're going to walk it out, work it out, in Jesus Mighty Name. Hallelujah, Glory to God!

Points to Remember:

- *Only one road leads to His truth*
- *We are anointed by the Spirit for purpose*
- *We are anointed to finish*
- *We have dominion*
- *We are wayfarers on the journey of truth*
- *Faith is our launching pad*
- *We are still in process*
- *We have to identify our gifts and operate in them*
- *We should invest in our vision*
- *We must recognize Kairos moments*
- *Success is deliberate*
- *Know your anointing*

www.ingramcontent.com/pod-product-compliance
Lightning Source LLC
Chambersburg PA
CBHW070614300426
44113CB00010B/1528